Appreciat

"This book traces the steps toward learning a new language and to discovering a culture other than one's own. In that quest, the author shows how one develops deeper insight about self along the way. This book is a must read and an inspiration for all."

—Justin Irish, *Spanish language learner and Assistant Superintendent, Edmonds School District, Washington*

"La autora ha escrito una historia excelente acerca de sus experiencias estudiando en Nicaragua y viviendo con una familia que la aceptó como miembro de la familia. Este libro le tocará el corazón."

—Jo Love Beach, *Profesora de español y residente de la Comunidad de Jubilados Panorama en Lacey, Washington*

"Este libro no es solamente una interesante narración de las experiencias y reflexiones de Penny; sino que es también testigo de que las relaciones interpersonales de confianza y respeto mutuo son esenciales para el desarrollo y aprendizaje del ser humano, en cualquier etapa y ámbito de la vida (incluyendo cuando se está aprendiendo un segundo idioma)."

—Annel Zuniga, *Nicaragüense y Coordinadora de Recursos Familiares, ChildStrive, Lynnwood, WA*

"This book is a most appropriately named one. As a person who has traveled and attempted to learn Spanish this book comes as a great comfort. Doing that is not easy, and yet, I would say everyone should do it. In this world, we need more bridges. Those will be built only by individuals, willing to risk, and to travel, and to put themselves in uncomfortable and unknown places. This book is a beautiful witness to just that."

—The Rt. Rev. Gregory H. Rickel, *the Diocese of Olympia, The Episcopal Church in Western Washington*

BRIDGING

Languages, Cultures and My Life

Penny Reid

Printed in the United States of America

First Printing, 2015

ISBN: 978-1-5186-0194-1

For orders, permissions, or requests, including special discounts for quantity purchases to schools and churches, please contact reidcooperative@gmail.com.

The content written by the author or contributors in this book is the sole opinion of that section's creator and does not necessarily represent the opinions or policies of the Edmonds School District (Lynnwood, Washington), Saint Mark's Episcopal Cathedral (Seattle, Washington), or the other organizations or companies included.

Developmental Editor and Designer:
Kristin Carroccino, www.carroccinocollective.com

English Copy Editor: Virginia Lenker
Spanish Copy Editor: Miriam C. Delgado
Proofreader: Linda Sollars

Cover Photo: Arjen Roersma, "Ernesto and Nohelia on Rio Tapasle Bridge," Near Muy Muy, Department of Matagalpa, Nicaragua. Used with permission from Arjen Roersma, Director of Matagalpa Tours.

Any clip art or other artwork not specifically credited is part of the public domain.

Proceeds from sales of this book will be given to organizations named herein.

For my family, on both sides of the bridge.

Para mi familia, en ambos lados del puente

✿CONTENTS✿

Clearly there are infinite acceptable ways to talk about what is Ineffable, that which is too great to describe fully. Likewise, there are many wonderful ways to practice peace and to create goodness.

—Penny Reid

International visitors helped separate the
coffee beans into groups when they visited the community of La Pita,
Nicaragua. (Photo by Bre Domescik)

*Visitantes extranjeros en la comunidad de La Pita, Nicaragua ayudaron a
separar en grupos los granos de café. (Foto de Bre Domescik)*

✿ Gratitude Gathering ✿

Author's Note: Every attempt was made to spell names correctly throughout the book but especially here. Also, several individuals could be listed over and over again in nearly every paragraph. I have only listed each person once, but in my heart and mind the warm gratitude expands and their names surface often. Finally, I have not included a glossary for the few Spanish words in this section because their meaning is obvious in context.

My friend asked me recently if I will be a more critical reader as a result of writing a book. Quite the opposite! I will be absolutely more appreciative whenever I pick up published reading material. Authoring a book is a giant task! I am fortunate there were many others with me.

I am especially grateful to my friends in Nicaragua who continue to demonstrate how to work together cooperatively. These people have a deep understanding, from birth, of what it means to be part of a team: Noelia Corrales, Freddy Membreño, Ernesto Ocampo, Nohelia Talavera, Maria Esperanza and Arjen Roersma.

Likewise I am totally in awe and thankful to my Nicaraguan sister-in-laughter, Marlene, and her husband, Joaquín, as well as their precious family members. They all welcomed me warmly as part of their clan, up-close-and-personal. Their care of me in every way makes me want to come home to Matagalpa again and again. I'm thinking fondly of Elsania and Ana, Walther and Yuri, Janett, Xiomara, and Lylian. And the children, thank God for them: Madelin, Fernando, Yuriana, Diego, María José, Herson, Janett and Eduardo. They create joy in their wake every day.

I am indebted to and love my teachers on both sides of the bridge wholeheartedly: Diana Iris Herrera Castro, Maria Jimenez, Susan Marshall and endless others, including but not limited to Marilyn, Ester, Xiomara, Yesica, Carla, Odelba and Lussiana. Natali and Patricia were also my gentle teachers. These women are all as patient and delightful as the day is long.

I am thankful for my neighbors—Lynn Edwards and Richard Robohm. These two let me tell the story of our 10 days together without edits and with generosity of spirit. Sarah Hornsby was another special guide I met while in Matagalpa. It has been sheer grace to share the writers' path with her in the lead.

I am very fortunate to have collected a wonderful group of fellow travelers and creators, including many who jumped at the chance to contribute and help me tell our story of Nicaragua, Nicaragüita. They met my deadlines and continued encouraging me: Betsy Bell, Marvin E. Chavarría M., John Daugherty, Bre Domescik, Ruth Harbaugh, Joyce Hedges, Ana Mesenbring, David Mesenbring and Ollie Mae Nicoll.

One fellow sojourner stands out: Jeanne Spurlock. She and I were pregnant at the same time eons ago when we lived across the houseboat dock from one another. She traveled with me twice to Nicaragua and knows my soul. She is my blessed amiga.

There were many readers who absorbed these pages early on when it was rough and gave me good, clear, honest feedback including Carla, Dick, Francis, Germán, Jane and Kali. They had my back. And Kerry and Julie in my Spanish circle helped too.

Thank Goodness for Jo Callaghan, my friend and jefa. She casually planted the idea for this book, "Maybe you can write about learning Spanish while you're there," and then put up with several sighs during this truly amazing year that started in Nicaragua. Another person I work with—Annie Rueda-Brown, my fellow school psychologist—certainly has my appreciation, as she helped me with translations and endless accommodations.

I am beholden to my editing team: Alfredo Feregrino, Virginia Lenker, Miriam C. Delgado and Linda Sollars. Kristin Carroccino—The Great—was my developmental editor and designer. She expanded my vision with simple words, "There is more story here," and then stood by me offering Brilliance and Talent every step of the way.

Grand thank yous and giant hugs for my prayer partner, my spiritual director and my chaplain. You know who you are.

I am blessed to have been born into a Sisterhood: me, Melissa and Susan. Now I think of my mother, Bernie, in that circle too. These beautiful steel magnolias whose blood I share are fine and varied examples of balanced strength.

I have two children I treasure: a son and a daughter, Clarke and Carolina. They both speak Spanish. They are patient with my slow and extroverted learning path. And both of them can write, teach and *make me laugh*. There is nothing better than being their mama.

There are two main men in my life: Rob, mi favorito marido who has been happily alongside me since we were young. That is saying something! And mi papá, John, a lover of words and books, will always be nearby for me. He was the first one to think the world of me and I am forever his daughter. Look, Dad, we did it!

Me and mi papá

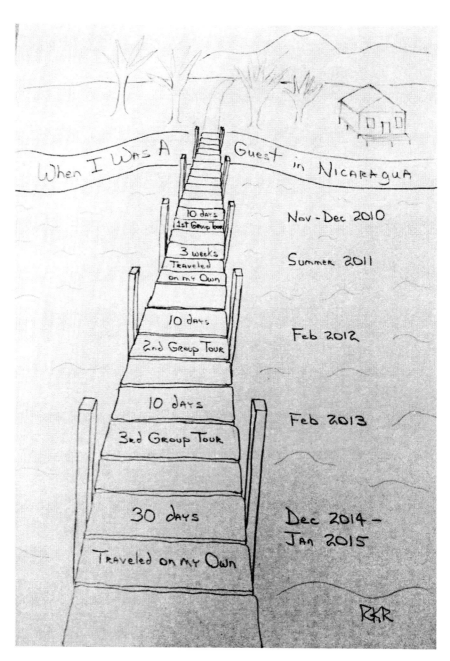

Illustrated by Rob Reid

✿ Introducción ✿

Why This? Why Now? Why Not?

Shortly before I returned to Nicaragua for my fifth visit, a colleague asked me, "Why are you going back there *again?*" Without thinking, I answered, "I don't completely know yet." Yes, I knew that I kept returning to Nicaragua to pursue a long-held goal to learn Spanish. I also knew that approximately 30 percent of the children I served—as an early childhood school psychologist in a district just north of Seattle—lived in homes where Spanish is spoken fluently. I knew that both of my young adult children spoke this second language well because they have lived in Spanish-speaking countries for extended periods of time. Because I participated regularly in a new urban bilingual congregation led by the first native-Spanish-speaking priest ordained in our Episcopal diocese, I also knew that I heard Spanish around me all the time.

As far as I was concerned, I couldn't learn it fast enough. Why wouldn't I keep going back?

But why specifically Nicaragua? I had chosen to return to this Spanish-speaking country in particular because I knew for a fact that these lovely, friendly people are patient with my slow learning rate. And there, English is not automatically spoken with North American tourists like it is in other places—Spain, for instance, and Costa Rica.

The first time I heard a language besides English spoken at length was the summer after I graduated from high school. For six weeks, I traveled in Mexico with a camp's youth group. Some of our time together was spent building a nursery in a small town, and usually we stayed at local churches. One week I experienced the thrill of my first homestay as the guest of a family in Mexico City. Fortunately I was paired with a confident peer who had studied Spanish in high school since I had only been exposed to French. All in all, when we returned home I was enamored with the language south of our border. The lyrical quality of different sounds combined to make deep meaning was like music to me. I could not help myself. Instead of satisfying my university's language requirement by passing a minimal proficiency test in French, I took two years of Spanish courses. Unfortunately, though, I didn't hear the language spoken by any native speakers at all.

Alas, after all that time I only had a minimal French-Spanish, two romance languages meshed together. Years later it was just sufficient enough to tell secrets to my husband Rob after our kids had learned to spell and we could no longer use the spelling method of clandestine communication between parents. That's about all my Franish was good for.

Enter my 50th birthday and Maria. She came into my life because her husband started serving as an assisting priest at our church, responsible for outreach ministries. My dream of learning Spanish flared again because Maria was born in Spain and I really liked her. I was intent on getting to know this bilingual speaker in our community. Since Maria was a preschool teacher, she knew how language is learned developmentally and understood how valuable respect and encouragement is to learners.

Together we constructed a beginning Spanish class for adults as well as a conversation class. We hired a sharp college student, Susan, to teach the beginners while Maria facilitated the conversation circle. We were off and running. Since I barely knew squat, I started in Susan's group and moved to Maria's as quickly as I could. After all, the lure of conversation always was and still is magnetic for me.

Since then I have looked for ways to improve my Spanish, mostly right here at home. I am not methodical. Organic is a better description. I tried starting a Spanish group over lunch at my old office where several employees were bilingual. I signed up for a community gathering of English and Spanish learners where half of our time was devoted to study in separate groups and half of the time to playing games and practicing together. On family vacations in Spanish-speaking countries, I bought magazines and CDs to practice reading and listening. While traveling, I always sat in the front seat with the van or taxi driver and tried to chat even though that sometimes led to confusion and/or hilarity for all.

Halfway into this concerted quest, we began inviting students from around the world to stay in our home. Travel as a family started us down the path, especially during my daughter Carolina's high school years, of welcoming others to stay with us for a few nights or weeks. Hosting international visitors opened the world to me in a new way.

I found that my Spanish leapt forward whenever I immersed myself. When Carolina was a junior, we decided to venture out on a homestay of our own. Rob, Carolina and I traveled to Guanajuato, Mexico, to study Spanish and live with a family for ten days—certainly not enough time to make much progress linguistically especially since I was traveling with English speakers and speaking English with them every chance I got. This was a vacation, after all. But I did build up some confidence during that stretch.

For all these experiences, I would still say my best Spanish study begins and ends in Nicaragua. When you bite off something as big as learning another language and realize how far away from mastering said task you actually are, you can get discouraged, believe me. What's more, you acknowledge that no matter how good you get, you'll never be able to speak without a foreign accent. Regardless, it's best to have friends on this quest and I happen to have found them in Nicaragua. Beautiful, brilliant, funny and endlessly accommodating friends.

My visits to Nicaragua started when Maria's husband David wanted to assemble a group of us to travel to Nicaragua in late 2010 to "see how most people live." I was interested. I reasoned that I liked the people in my church and this could be a way to improve my Spanish. Besides, I could take time off from work using my personal days. I would be studying microcredit, politics and the like. I was in.

That initial trip to Nicaragua was the first time I had traveled internationally without Rob. I had not done much exploring in developing countries, at least not in the developing parts of them, and not in Nicaragua at all, reportedly one of the poorest countries in our hemisphere. (See

Appendix A for detailed demographics about Nicaragua.) Those ten days, I even slept with my money belt on, my passport carefully zipped inside. My passport still has part of the money belt melted onto it, thanks to my sweat and grime. Talk about paranoid!

During that first trip, while in Matagalpa in the mountains of Nicaragua, we met social-entrepreneur Noelia Corrales. We enjoyed meeting her so much that we travelers invited her to come to Seattle for a speaking tour to help us tell others what we'd learned while in her country. The following summer, I spent two weeks on my own studying at her language school in Matagalpa and, for the first time, lived with Marlene, Joaquín and their beautiful Nicaraguan family. In later years I participated in two more study tours sponsored by our church.

I have journeyed to Nicaragua with each of my family members—Rob, Carolina and son Clarke. Besides Noelia, we have also hosted Spanish speakers from Peru and Nicaragua to educate our friends about microcredit as we party down together. Every time I connect with these friends, my Spanish improves and I rekindle my relationships. (For a good description of how powerful the microcredit business model can be, please see Appendix B, an annual report from Aldea Global sent to St. Mark's Episcopal Cathedral to account for the Cathedral's contributions to help Nicaraguan women create and develop small businesses. The report chronicles a year's worth of small loans to business owners.)

Imagine my delight when I discovered a way to legitimately return to Nicaragua for a solid month during the easier-for-travelers dry season. I combined my personal leave, winter vacation time and the school district's version of a sabbatical—one week of short leave. My boss suggested I write while in Nicaragua about learning Spanish through immersion as part of a "senior project," which is my employer's way of compensating leaders who have reached the top of the salary schedule. Through this allocation the school district contributes to the professional development of staff members for the benefit of students, families and the wider community. As it turned out, instead of completing this text in return for my senior project stipend, I created several Spanish documents that I use at work, including an Early Childhood Spanish-English Glossary. (See Appendix C.)

But now as I write, I sometimes scare myself because I wonder if mine is an unfolding story that never seems quite baked or good enough. Is it really worthy of the pages in a book? After all, I did not return from my fifth visit fluent and ready to share my story of grand success through persistence. But then I lead a tour of the preschool where I work and two thirds of those participating, including the interpreter, are Spanish-speakers. And I can chat with them some in both languages. The one Nicaraguan father I'd worked with in the eight years I've been in the district called me before my recent trip asking for assistance, even though I hadn't talked with him in three years. Another friend in Matagalpa, sent an email before the trip asking me to intercept and transport the binoculars he'd ordered through the internet. My language-learning-forever path was and continues to be confirmed over and over again.

Certainly I am part of a web as I stand on this link bridging two cultures, two languages and two countries. I still "code switch," using two languages in the same message as I speak and write. But I find that as I learn Spanish I am stretching my mind and heart to its maximum, a worthy experience every time it happens. The goal is that my Spanish improves, the code switching decreases and I can cross the bridge from one side to the other more fluently. And through my story, I want to encourage others who are learning Spanish. A working middle-aged woman *can* communicate and continue to learn. We'll see what else is in store. I am sure to be surprised and delighted.

The Core of Who I Am

I want you know where I'm coming from with all of these references to church and priests and such. By including these words, I may risk alienating some readers. Simply put, I could not tell this story and leave those words out. If you get a little nervous when religion comes up, don't worry. I have been working in public schools long enough to know how unnecessarily complicated religion can make things. For example, thirty years ago I was scolded by the fundamentalists for teaching breathing techniques to test-anxious kids. So I get a little nervous too, even though then, as well as now, I profoundly respect and live out, the separation of church and state at work.

Still, I've decided I can't live divided any more, especially when I'm writing about learning Spanish. I was born into a particular faith language and as much exploring as I've done outside of it, for me personally, these words— prayer, cathedral, etc—are central.

In my heart of hearts, I stand on the bridge. Sometimes I *am* the bridge. From here, I can see two sides, at least two sides, to most of my life experiences. I studied special education imbedded in general education. I lived in a world dominated by black and white, then gray and brown. I speak English, studied French and am learning Spanish. I serve both children and grown-ups in my work life. I am a psychologist, thus both artist and scientist. Even politically and spiritually, I can inhabit all sides of the aisles. And, get this: on day one, I was proclaimed both dead, then alive. Specifically, while my mother was in labor, the obstetrician told my father I was dead. Later when I started screaming, that doctor had to eat his words.

So apart from whatever religious language I may use, I have become an ally, an advocate, usually for the minority and what may not be obvious to us, the privileged ones. Not loudly and very actively but with a deep understanding of what it means to be visibly different, unusual, underdog. I convene others in community so that everyone gets heard, and usually appreciated, often loved. I need and want to speak Spanish so I can get to know others better and walk alongside.

Even from a place of ambiguity, poverty, injustice or very sheer grief and sadness, I am rarely completely silent. I continue to breathe. I tend to see hope and promise anyway. I am profoundly optimistic, even when it comes to learning a second language in middle age. Always have been—after all, I grew up knowing I had overcome death itself—always will be.

Guidance to Readers

The backbone of this book is a journal recorded when I traveled to Nicaragua on my own to study Spanish for 30 days. To show what happens in the learner's mind as the second language becomes more accessible and conversational I have intentionally included more and more Spanish words as the days progress. Thus the first form of code switching you'll encounter in this book—using more than one language in the same episode of communication.

A second type of code switching occurred while I was in Nicaragua because my father was dying. I often found myself pondering the language of death in the midst of intense life. The bookend entries, titled "Before" and "After," provide context about my state of mind and heart at the time. The reality of my dad's passing definitely added a sense of aliveness and urgency to my experience of the learning and loving in community that is described in these bookend sections.

Organizationally, each daily entry starts with the day's number and a title in English. Next a key word is translated, followed by a Tip of the Day which is elaborated on, directly or indirectly, in the diary paragraphs that follow. A photo is also included with a caption in Spanish.

Even if you don't know much Spanish, you can try to understand the photo caption and Spanish words by studying the photo or using other contextual clues in the writing. This is not unlike how we all learned our first language. However if using context alone proves too frustrating, a glossary is included near the end of each day's material. It contains the translation of the photo caption as well as the new words or phrases from Spanish into English that have been introduced in the most recent entry. Any given word will only appear in the book's glossary lists once, and it will show up in the order and form found in the text. For example, adjectives will appear as masculine or feminine. Verbs will be conjugated as they are in the written language.

Most daily entries also include a special supplement elaborating on the journal content. These additions may be poems, data, recipes, essays or artwork by the author or others. If the contribution was originally submitted totally in Spanish, the translation will follow directly in English. If there are only a few new Spanish words, these words will be translated and included in the glossary.

While the Spanglish journal entries may be too choppy or confusing for some readers, hopefully this steady layout for all 30 entries will help.

☼Before☼

Hermanitos en mi primera casa en Managua

These two beautiful boys were part of the first Nicaraguan family I stayed with five years ago. I spoke very little Spanish then and was welcomed into their modest open-air home where I would soon learn that fellow pilgrim Ana and I would be sharing a twin bed for the night, apparently the only bed in the house. These two children along with Ana, then age 13, made this shocking news and humble lodging bearable and, eventually, joyous for me. We discovered games we could all play together and laughed ourselves silly with these two. At one point, the older fellow held my face in his hands, looked solemnly at me and stated, in hushed amazement, "Tus ojos son celestes." Ana helped me decipher the meaning. Together we realized "celeste" must come from the same roots as our English word "celestial." The sky blue he was raving about was heavenly—and the color of my eyes—and I felt blessed and safe in his hands.

When it came time to travel back to Nicaragua for my 30-day leave at Christmastime, it was especially important to conjure up confirming memories like this one. My father at 94 had been receiving hospice care for almost two years and, given my deep connection to family and to him in particular, it became hard to follow through on this dream of immersion for Spanish study. Even though I had spent more than a year creating my plan, I recognized he might die while I was gone. It helped that he had always lived life to the fullest and encouraged me to go. As an educator himself, he knew it was a near miracle that I had permission to be away for a full month in the middle of the school year and had somehow found a way to get my work covered (I had an excellent intern!). Plus he was curious about the writing project since he had recently published his own memoirs. In general, Dad was still acting like he'd live forever to help me take the chance of missing his exit.

Before this I hadn't had a lot of experience with death. I had witnessed it once before when we were traveling in Kenya and came upon a car accident. The woman was lying on the dusty roadside, injured with a bright trickle of blood running from her nose. The circle of Germans and Canadians and Americans and Masai had begun to form, the vultures whirled overhead, and the ER doctor who happened to be along for the ride pronounced her dead.

My dear Rob had lost two brothers as well as his parents and I had grieved alongside him. I had also weathered some tough diagnoses with dear ones. Our dog Roxy had had mast cell cancer at age 5 and my sister faced lymphoma at age 25. But Roxy was old, almost 13, when I was packing for my trip to Nicaragua and my sister, well, she was robustly healthy at 55.

All in all, as tough as it was to leave my Dad, just as it had been when I faced death and disease of loved ones in the past, his predicament had the odd impact of making me Wake Up and Be Present. I was going to a land of great loss, suffering and poverty, some significantly exacerbated by my own country. I had also experienced the vibrant color and brilliant creativity of Nicaragua's people plus her exquisite natural diversity. And I had dear friends there. In part *because* my father was dying I returned to Nicaragua intent on grabbing Life every way I could and sharing Love at its deepest and fullest, including writing about what I learned. This seemed a fitting way to honor my father even if it was to be my final farewell.

Nicaragua: From the Eyes of a Teenager

By Ana Mesenbring, 13, (Nicaragua delegate 2010)

It's about 9:00 p.m. Nicaragua time, as my fellow delegates and I step off our final flight after a long day of traveling. I expect to feel relief as I step off the stuffy plane, only to have a wave of hot, humid, sticky air welcome me to the long awaited Nicaragua. My first thoughts are, "OH MY GOD what am I doing here!" All I can do is complain for what seems like an eternity as we wait for our luggage, climb aboard a crowded bus, arrive at our stay for that night and plunge into the coldest shower of my life. You may think that a cold shower might feel "refreshing" after being in such weather, but believe me, it did not. "Welcome to Nicaragua," I thought as I watched bugs crawl and listened to my roommates snoring later that night, "It's gonna be a long trip."

Things didn't look up much until I had gotten through the morning lectures and meetings, and went on our first outing into the bustling and exciting city of Managua. That's when I began to get excited. Why? I really don't know since there was not a clothing store in sight. As I was pondering this question, a young man who appeared to be in need of money jumped onto the hood of our van and fervently began washing its windows. I froze in my seat, for I had never seen anything like it. There were cars honking and traffic piling up behind us, but the man did not cease his washing. When he finished and our tour guide paid him, he immediately began washing the back windows. Though the majority of the group waved it off and moved on, I was astonished. Looking back on it now, I realize that this experience was just the beginning of my strange encounters with the amazing people of Nicaragua.

Compañera

We didn't just interact with the people by day, and then go to a hotel at night. No, we actually went into the homes of Nicaraguans for four entire nights. The fact that they would send us into the homes of complete strangers, in my case, without my Dad to hide behind, was just cruel. The good thing though, was I wasn't completely alone. I had the fearless, hilarious, anything but shy, Penny Reid, as my "compañera" or "roommate." I had my doubts about these homestays before, but never more than when we were led through the dark streets of this little "barrio" by a little boy of 8 years ... and his mother.

Penny, of course, was already laughing and conversing with this little boy, while I was scared to death. I found myself surprised when we finally stopped at a small house with a metal gate for a door. Inside was a perfect family setting: a father in a big chair laughing with his family on the couch next to him. Despite the conditions of their furniture (roadside worthy), they all seemed perfectly content. Their conversation and laughter came to a halt as Penny and I walked through the "doorway." It suddenly resumed as they jumped up and welcomed us into their home. The stories and memories they shared are ones you would never hear while sipping red wine with a rich couple in America. I was beginning to see that maybe homestays weren't such a cruel idea after all.

After a simple meal of rice and beans (that appeared to be surprisingly good when you mix it with amazing people and lively conversation), we were led to our living quarters which turned out to be a twin "bed" in some sort of room that by night was the bedroom of a 15-year-old, and by day was a storage room for miscellaneous baby clothes and toys. The man who led us to our room, a son in the family who was visiting from Costa Rica where he works in a touristy hotel, said in broken English, "Many Americans who come through the hotel where I work would never be able to fit on this bed."

When you can't see the staircase

We not only slept in this bed, but in many other "beds" in a country where the word "privacy" does not, I repeat not, exist. Many times we lay at night questioning whether we were sharing a bed with a family of bedbugs, but reminded ourselves we need to push away from our fears, whether those fears were of dogs sneaking into the occupied latrine with no door, or worrying about our family back home. The Martin Luther King Jr. quote, "Faith is taking the first step even when you can't see the whole staircase" defiantly carried me through this amazing trip. From my journal entry on the first day, "Wow this sucks" to the one on the last day, "I'm so glad I came on this trip, it feels like I have another family now—my Nica family," I feel that this trip was to say the least, transformative. What I saw in Nicaragua is what every American teenager would never want to see, but definitely needs to see.

GLOSSARY

CAPTION = LITTLE BROTHERS IN MY FIRST HOME IN MANAGUA

CELESTE = SKY BLUE
COMPAÑERA = ROOMMATE
BARRIO = NEIGHBORHOOD

Day 1—Traveling

BRIDGE = EL PUENTE

TIP OF THE DAY: **CHOOSE IMMERSION.**

Lindas plantas en el patio de Marlene

I am on a plane heading to Nicaragua for the fifth time in as many years. I am curious to see what will happen if I allow myself to only write a few paragraphs in English each day. My Spanish is rough at best, and I want to continue living in Seattle with a job and husband I love, so I only have a short time away. I'm not staying for several months—the time it took my own children to become fluent Spanish speakers. I'll be returning home in a month—minimal immersion experience, at best. But complete immersion, no matter how short, *can* make a difference and will happen if I choose Spanish as the language to use whenever possible. For instance, I've decided to write my usual journal notes in Spanish when I can, likely peppered with Spanglish of course. I brought my Spanish Bible along. I have already started striking up conversations with willing Spanish-speaking travelers, my seatmate on the flight from Atlanta to Managua being a great example.

Still, I am decidedly on el puente, one foot solidly in both languages and really feeling like the gringo I am. These musings are not about vocabulary, grammar or conjugations. Rather I intend to describe how a beginning conversationalist can transform to using intermediate receptive and expressive levels as I live it. I came to this project with many of the basics. I can count in Spanish. I know the colors and the names of family members. I know one word for most things. All in all, I know many more than 50 words so I am able to put three to five words together in a sentence, por ejemplo. Frankly, I am similar to the preschoolers I know through work—preschool Spanish is mine. Mostly, on this trip, I would like to let go of translating every word. Instead, I want to let the language roll over and around me, happy to understand the gist and more and more often the precise message.

Memorandum

From David Mesenbring

Author's Note: My first trip to Nicaragua in 2010 was with a group from Saint Mark's Episcopal Cathedral in Seattle, my church home. The Cathedral's relationship with Nicaragua is described below through excerpts from a memorandum dated 10/12/09. The memo was from the Reverend David Mesenbring to Saint Mark's Church in the World (CIW) Coordinating Committee.

Historical Background

Saint Mark's unusually strong ministry focus on Nicaraguan solidarity dates back to the 1980's. While it involved some painful lessons, our relationship with the rural barrio "adopted" for nutritional enhancement also afforded the highly positive opportunity for transformational travel by cathedral members, including the youth choir pilgrimage and several other trips. An annual dinner drew hundreds in support of the Nicaraguan Education and Health Assistance Project (NEHAP). The Jubilee Northwest ministry is a highly successful outgrowth of NEHAP's work. In 2003, the Cathedral received a bequest in support of NEHAP's mission. By 2007, nearly all NEHAP leaders had transferred to other parishes and the group formally came to the end of its organizational life cycle.

Through critical reflection on some good lessons learned, CIW leaders have evolved a sophisticated understanding of the potential for reconstructing a Nicaraguan ministry focused on God's call to us for transformation of both the "servants" and "served" alike. Throughout 2008, CIW staff and volunteer leaders worked on how best to honor the 2003 bequest in a manner which could revive a reformed Nicaraguan ministry. In early 2009, the Vestry approved our proposal that NEHAP's remaining funds be given to Aldea Global, a cooperative of farmers in Jinotega, in order to establish a microloan fund benefiting women engaged in sustainable agriculture. A Memo of Understanding defining the terms of this gift commits Aldea Global to coordinating visits to Jinotega by Saint Mark's. ... Recently we learned that our gift has devolved into several new loans.

Next Steps

The Cathedral's new Strategic Plan includes a target...that embodies a long held goal of the CIW Coordinating Committee to seek transformation of the world and ourselves via travel among people whose material circumstances differ radically from our own. ... I am prepared to travel ... in furtherance of your view that a preliminary journey is needed to communicate with Aldea Global's leadership about the unconventional nature of our pilgrimage objectives focused on helping Nicaraguans by transforming our own worldview.

GLOSSARY

CAPTION = LOVELY PLANTS ON MARLENE'S PATIO

POR EJEMPLO = FOR EXAMPLE

Day 2—Managua

REST = EL DESCANSO

TIP OF THE DAY: **RELAX.**

Las velas de Adviento en una Iglesia Episcopal en Managua

In Nicaragua, people say, "Tranquila." I often hear the word directed at me as a one-word suggestion which I take to mean, "Relax." The same colleague who asked me why I was returning to Nicaragua, asked me, "So is that word a combination of tranquil and tequila?" Sí, that's a good way to remember it.

This time I chose to stay in Managua for the first night. On other trips, after I arrived around 8:30 p.m., a driver from Matagalpa Tours met me, and we hightailed it up the Pan American Highway for two-plus hours and arrived at my host family's home at midnight. This time though, I had the wherewithal to spring for a hotel. Talk about being on the bridge, actually stepping right back into my comfort zone. But not a bad way to offload a hundred bucks. Too bad I had worried about how I would get to the hotel (which was, by the way, in walking distance from the airport). Who says Nicaragua is not "developed." At the airport and with tourist dollars to spend, I admit I was The Tourist—so much for immersion. After immigration and customs, right as I stepped into baggage claim, I saw my name on a gentleman's placard. He whisked me with my bags right across the street to Las Mercedes Best Western. I marveled at the ease of it all, remembering my first night four years ago in Managua with my fellow travelers from church when all I saw from baggage claim was a wall of faces waiting on the outside to offer me a taxi or to greet their loved one. Last night the entire scene was tranquila and I was simply amazed and pinching myself.

Another item I wasted time fretting about was la misa. Because I was in Managua on Sunday morning as well as the specific day during the year for honoring The Virgin of Guadalupe, I wanted to go to mass at the Episcopal cathedral. Over the years I have appreciated times when I have honored Sabbath, a day of descanso and relaxation at the end of an otherwise busy week. On this blessed Sunday, my Nicaraguan/U.S. citizen amiga, Carla, picked me up and drove me across town to church. After desayuno together at the hotel's buffet (and my first nacatamale this time around), we ventured forth. What a gift! Things I treasured about being with Carla included:

+ The opportunity to speak fluidly in English.
+ The chance to have a ready translator alongside.
+ Time in the car together to share our lives.
+ An experienced escort who learned to drive safely (somehow) in Managua.
+ The chance to compare notes and debrief alone after encounters.

Another comfort was finding the Anglican/Episcopal service I have come to know and love. And even though it was completely in Spanish at least I could join in during El Padre Nuestro, one of the two poems I have memorized in my lifetime (the other being The Lord's Prayer in English). Gratefully, I feel rested and ready to head to Matagalpa esta mañana.

El Padre Nuestro

Padre nuestro que estás en el cielo,
santificado sea tu Nombre,
venga tu reino,
hágase tu voluntad,
en la tierra como en el cielo.
Danos hoy nuestro pan de cada día.
Perdona nuestras ofensas,
como también nosotros perdonamos
a los que nos ofenden.
No nos dejes caer en tentación
y libranos del mal.
Porque tuyo es el reino,
tuyo es el poder,
y tuya es la gloria,
ahora y por siempre. Amén.

The Lord's Prayer
Our Father in heaven,
hallowed be your Name,
your kingdom come,
your will be done,
on earth as in heaven.
Give us today our daily bread.
Forgive us our sins
as we forgive those
who sin against us.
Save us from the time of trial
and deliver us from evil.
For the kingdom, the power,
and the glory are yours,
now and forever. Amen.

GLOSSARY

CAPTION=THE CANDLES OF ADVENT AT AN EPISCOPAL CHURCH IN MANAGUA

TRANQUILA = CALM, RELAXED

SÍ = YES

LA MISA = MASS

AMIGA = FRIEND

DESAYUNO = BREAKFAST

NACATAMALE = NICARAGUAN TAMALE

ESTA MAÑANA = THIS MORNING

Day 3—Marlene's House

Marlene me bendecía tres veces al día con comidas deliciosas.

I am already recognizing a pattern here; like at home, I am writing first thing in the morning. Unlike at home where I journal privately, here I am imagining readers. I am editing and trying to force it all to make sense. Another difference from my usual morning practice time is I have una mezcla of thoughts and ideas which, de verdad, are un poco locas. Fortunately at least, dormí bien.

And with that, I am back to the topic of the day: Gifting. I can hear Marlene—blessed Marlene—laughing, deep in her throat and with her mouth closed so it is quiet, outside my window where presumably, she is washing clothes by hand. It is the dry season after all, so running a machine might be not just inefficient but downright impossible.

I am remembering the first time I was in Nicaragua, under the wing of an organization called Witness for Peace. We were strictly told not to give anything to our hosts. Offering tangible gifts is the usual North American response and it complicates relationships, we were told. Instead we agreed to receive, to be the guests. To give only love and interest. To be curious, and, therefore, give curiosity. Ah. To be interested and therefore give interest. To be loving and therefore give love. And it was enough ... very pure, in fact, and a new way of being for those of us who have so much in the material sense.

This time it is Christmas though, and my culture and traditions are different and run so deep in me. Yesterday for instance was Clarke's birthday and my first birthing day. I took un regalo to class—aplets y cotlets—in honor of my son, like the hobbits do. They give gifts instead of getting them on their birthdays. I enjoyed this and my teacher seemed to as well. Still, I miss my early days in Nicaragua when someone else defined exactly what I was to bestow, how much and how. This land of propinas is awkward especially when I consider mi amiga Marlene. Of course, after I stay at a hotel, use a tourist van or get a cup of café, I always leave a tip. I can only imagine at this point, en amistad, my best advice to myself is, "Flow." Big, open heart, receiving freely, giving freely.

A Cure for Blindness?

By David Mesenbring

Author's Note: The following excerpts are from a sermon preached by the Reverend David Mesenbring at Saint Mark's Cathedral on the third Sunday in Advent—December 12, 2010—after our first Transformational Travel tour in Nicaragua. They inform my thoughts about giving.

A dozen of us just returned from Nicaragua where we spent the first ten days of Advent working on [a] target of our strategic plan: "*Offer members of the Cathedral community more opportunities to travel amongst peoples whose circumstances are different from our own, and to be transformed by this experience."* For two nights, we split into pairs to stay with families in a Managua barrio where homes may not have more than one small bed. We visited rural areas and studied microfinance as well as U.S.-Nicaraguan history, economics, and trade. Our first day started with a bible study contrasting friendship and strangership [reading Luke 24:13–49]. Late in the trip, at our daily reflection together, one poetic pilgrim suggested we had caught "a virus of inspiration."...

... In a small Nicaraguan town not frequented by tourists, we met a crusty, old gringo who had been kicking around Central America for decades. He presumed we were yet another U.S. church group on some service mission we hoped would be of some help. Crossing our path in the hallway of a tiny hotel, he blurted out, "These people don't need any help!" But our mission was not as he expected. We'd come to work on our own blindness about how most people live. A 'service project' would have felt good compared with the shame we experienced as we learned history our society's deaf to. ...

...Is the hope of our relatively rich church in sync with this world's poor majority? Travel designed to transform the traveler's blindness resists a high horse of charitable largesse that North Americans like to ride. Service projects might make us feel good but presume a certain superiority that is not the best posture for learning. ...

... Western Christians have practiced only half of the mission God gives us. Focusing on the gifts we want to share can obscure the gifts others offer us. Some of those gifts match needs we don't even know we have! At the end of our trip, we made three lists. One lists 90 strangers who we met. A second contains 95 types of gifts we think those strangers might offer us. The third brainstorms how to share those gifts among the communities we return home to.

GLOSSARY

CAPTION = MARLENE BLESSED ME THREE TIMES EACH DAY WITH DELICIOUS MEALS.

UNA MEZCLA = A MIXTURE

DE VERDAD = TRUTHFULLY

UN POCO LOCAS = A LITTLE CRAZY

DORMÍ BIEN. = I SLEPT WELL.

Y = AND

PROPINAS = TIPS

MI = MY

CAFÉ = COFFEE

EN AMISTAD = IN FRIENDSHIP

Day 4—Interlude

USA = EEUU

TIP OF THE DAY: **LEARN A DIFFERENT WAY.**

En la Nicaragua tropical, las flores de Pascua crecen naturalmente en los jardines, el campo y la selva tropical. (Foto de Bre Domescik)

Something odd has happened. When I returned home and reread my little diario through, I realized one entry was missing. I'd only written for 29 days and I'd been traveling for 30. Since I have considered writing more from home anyway, I am going to place something here, as an interlude.

I have been home for less than three weeks and I have learned that it's not advisable to use this booklet for my senior project at work because I might want to copyright it. So here I stand on the bridge, wondering if this piece really could be useful and encouraging to someone else who has taken on this rewarding and difficult task of learning Spanish. Is my unorthodox Spanglish presentation too rough on the reader's mind, let alone mine? When I share journal-like comments, am I simply stroking my own ego?

This break does provide another opportunity to warn you, sweet reader. Since the mix of languages increases intentionally, you might want to stop now. How I wish I could say that when you reach Day 30, you will be reading my fluent Spanish. But that won't happen. I encourage you to rely less and less (or not at all?) on the glossaries and see if you can understand the gist of my story anyway.

Are you willing to acknowledge the increasing amount of Spanish language circulating around you in the EEUU and try to understand some of it? Maybe my treatise will allow you a window into the mind of the Spanish-speaking man you see sometimes at church who is finally beginning to include a few words of English as he speaks. Or it will encourage you to connect to a mother who desperately wants to communicate with you but would rather not appear foolish. She is embarrassed by her developing English. But when you deliver some of your rough Spanish, all of a sudden, like magic, you are conversing about her child and both sharing your concerns and solutions.

Back to the other side of the bridge now. Hopefully we can return to entries written in Nicaragua with fresh questions and motivation to guide us.

"Adiós"

By Clarke Reid

Author's Note: For the past three years, my son, Clarke, has taught in Spanish-speaking towns and cities, including Pozoblanco, Andalusia in Spain. Talk about immersion! His Spanish is now fluent. At one of the schools he described the meaning of "Adiós" and how the word is sometimes used on the streets. "Adiós" is often used in Nicaragua in passing and, given the change-up journal topic for Day 4, this seemed as good as any place to insert his comments and translation.

"Adiós" es una palabra que muchos estudiantes aprenden cuando comienzan a estudiar la lengua española (aunque en algunos países de Latino América, ha sido reemplazada casi completamente por otras palabras, como "chau".) Se suele traducir en "goodbye" pero una mejor traducción sería "farewell" o "godspeed," porque la palabra es una contracción de "a dios," lo cual significa literalmente, "to god." Es claramente un vestigio de hace siglos, cuando toda la vida en España se motivaba por el Cristianismo, pero es aún muy común hoy en día. En Pozoblanco, no es solo una despedida, es una estrategia indispensable para saludar. ¿Quieres decir "hello" y "goodbye" en una sola palabra? Adiós es tu palabra. ...

Con "Adiós" (o "ayó" como suena en el acento murmurado pero expresivo de Andalucía) puedes saludar amigablemente a conocidos que pasen en la calle sin enrollarte en una conversación larga. "Adiós" dice "hello," "I hope you have a good day [Espero que tengas un buen día]," y "goodbye" en una simple palabra.

"Adios"

"Adios" is a word most people learn very early when studying Spanish (even though in some Latin American countries like Chile and Argentina, it is almost entirely replaced by other words, like "chau.") Usually it is translated as "goodbye" but a better translation might be "farewell" or "godspeed" because it is a contraction of "a dios" which literally means "to god." Clearly it is a relic of centuries ago when life in Spain revolved around Christianity but it is still very common today. In Pozoblanco, it's not only a farewell, but an indispensable greeting tool. Ever wanted to say "hello" and "goodbye" to someone at the same time? Adios is your word. ...

With "Adios" (or "ayó" as it sounds through the mumbled but expressive Andalusian accent) you can amicably acknowledge passing acquaintances without involving yourself in a full conversation. "Adios" says "Hello," "I hope you have a good day," and "goodbye" all in one simple word.

GLOSSARY

CAPTION = IN TROPICAL NICARAGUA, POINSETTAS GROW WILD IN GARDENS, THE COUNTRYSIDE AND RAIN FORESTS. (PHOTO BY BRE DOMESCIK)

DIARIO = DIARY

Day 5—Code Switching

¡Que manera de empezar el día!

Quizás my lot is to sleep well only every other night because as I write this morning about yesterday, I did *not* sleep "well" last night. Actually, if you'll indulge me for a moment, dulce lectora, I did not sleep *long*. Usually I get a good solid four or five deep hours before waking for my nightly trip to the bathroom. Last night I didn't go back to sleep after peeing but stayed awake because the cock started crowing. All the more reason to revel in the long luxurious eight hour stretches when they do come—and they did, in my not too distant memory as witnessed by the words I wrote to introduce this day's entry: Dormí bien. Una mezcla, sí? ¡Es complicada, de verdad!

I do notice already that the results of code switching are happening. Sometimes when I try to pull up a relatively easy English word (por ejemplo, "catheter" or "burlesque"), it's just not there. And I'm not talking about the slowness of middle age memory but rather the nature of learning a second language. Children have the same experience and sometimes as professionals, we erroneously question their basic intelligence because while learning English, a child's ability to fluidly communicate in his or her first language diminishes. I am experiencing this phenomenon myself, as I live and breathe.

I do have very fond memories of yesterday. My weekdays start with three hours of one-on-one lessons at the school. While there and with the sweet breath of a grand night's sleep buoying me, I read un ensayo interesante about Virginia Wolfe en la mañana con mi maestra, Diana, and enjoyed a long break for lunch and una siesta at Marlene's. Then I returned to school for the highlight of the day. It was a cooking lesson under the tutelage of Estercita. We made plantain empanadas together and chatted away, as friends do while cooking. Throughout the day I was surprised and delighted at my feelings of calm reassurance. Poco a poco, the Spanish is coming. Definitely un milagro. I keep pinching myself as I am contentedly living my dream.

The bonus of waking early was finding on my bedside table Nicaraguan poet Pablo Antonio Cuadra's *Book of Hours*, translated into English by Sarah Hornsby and Matthew C. Hornsby. In the prologue, I was delighted to find a reference to Nohelia, a friend and guía Matagalpina whom I traveled with during an earlier trip. Dare I say, "Small world?" I am convinced that, as the meta-physicists explain, all is connected. To embrace this understanding, I come to Nicaragua, Nicaragüita regularly.

Receta Tortitas De Plátano Maduro

INGREDIENTES:
PLÁTANOS MADUROS
QUESO RALLADO
ACEITE PARA FREÍR

PROCESO:
1. CORTAR LOS PLÁTANOS EN TROZOS Y PONERLOS A COCER (CON LA CASCARA)
2. PELAR Y MAJAR LOS PLÁTANOS HASTA HACERLOS PURE
3. SOBRE UN MOLDE DE PLÁSTICO HACER PEQUEÑAS TORTILLAS, PONER QUESO RALLADO Y PLÁTANOS EN EL CENTRO Y DOBLAR POR LA MITAD, CERRANDO BIEN LOS BORDES
4. FREÍR EN UN POCO DE ACEITE, VOLTEAR CUANDO CADA LADO ESTÉ DORADO
5. SACARLAS DE LA SARTÉN Y SERVIR. NOTA: SE PUEDEN DISFRUTAR CON ENSALADA O CREMA DULCE.

Recipe for Ripe Plantain Tortitas

INGREDIENTS:
RIPE PLANTAINS
GRATED CHEESE
OIL FOR FRYING

DIRECTIONS:
1. CUT THE PLANTAINS IN CHUNKS AND COOK THEM (IN THE SKINS).
2. PEEL AND MASH THE PLANTAINS UNTIL PURÉED.
3. ON A PLASTIC MOLD, MAKE SMALL TORTILLAS, PUT GRATED CHEESE AND PLANTAINS IN THE CENTER AND FOLD EACH TORTILLA IN HALF, SEALING THE BORDERS WELL.
4. FRY IN A LITTLE OIL, TURNING WHEN EACH SIDE IS GOLDEN.
5. TAKE THEM OUT OF THE FRYING PAN AND SERVE. ... *NOTE*: THESE CAN BE ENJOYED WITH SALAD OR SWEET CREAM.

GLOSSARY

CAPTION = WHAT A WAY TO START THE DAY!

QUIZÁS = PERHAPS

DULCE LECTORA = SWEET READER

ES COMPLICADA = IT'S COMPLICATED

VERDAD = TRUE

UN ENSAYO = AN ESSAY

INTERESANTE = INTERESTING

CON = WITH

MAESTRA = TEACHER

UNA SIESTA = A NAP

POCO A POCO = LITTLE BY LITTLE

UN MILAGRO = A MIRACLE

GUÍA = GUIDE

MATAGALPINA = MATAGALPIAN

NICARAGÜITA = LITTLE NICARAGUA

Day 6—A Steep Path

TIP OF THE DAY: **TAKE CARE.**

Los escalones hacia la casa de Marlene y Joaquín

There is una colina I know well in Matagalpa; it's outside la casa de Marlene—mi casa nicaragüense. It is quite steep and I traverse it at the very beginning or very end of my 15-minute walk to and from the school. When I reach the top, for descanso midday and then again at the end of my school day I release the bolt in the tall metal gate that clangs and announces my arrival. Each time I am welcomed with open arms. I pass through a small patio garden that peeks out on a view of the mountains with the city below. Usually someone is rocking one of the babies in el próximo salón pequeño. No one gets up or changes the course of the conversation or their lives, but I feel enveloped here nonetheless. I can rest and I can laugh or cry. I even have my own room and bathroom. And Marlene is a fabulous cook. When I sit down for a meal made with her hands, I am flooded with warm gratitude.

All of which are infinite gifts for me knowing that there is also a hill in my mind and heart here in Matagalpa as I attempt to learn Spanish. And I found it yesterday in a steep way. Fitting that it was Wednesday, "hump day." I scared myself with thoughts of how hard this is and how lonely I feel sometimes. That I would dare to come here at Christmastime. That I would come immediately from a full workweek to "foreign soil."

Thank God I had the wherewithal to choose to stay in this very home with Marlene and her beautiful family. Lloro ahora because I am profoundly touched and grateful.

I also had the wisdom to schedule a 30-minute massage at Armonía yesterday. For 200 córdobas [less than $10(US)], I relaxed quietly con Patricia en las manos gentle de Patricia. Afterwards I was open to the activity at Escuela Colibrí, watching a bittersweet movie about a woman who is blind and discussing it afterwards with my afternoon teacher, Marilyn.

Risas flowed again at Marlene's as we shared the stories of our days and the humor of language and this often absurd task I've taken on.

Mi Corazón Lleno,
Pocas Palabras Para Describir Mi Pecado

Author's Note: I am still processing the moment during our second group tour when I separated from our group in a public market in León and a man asked me if I was Nicaraguan. A bit puffed up with pride in my meager Spanish, I explained I was from the U.S. and watched him turn on me. In my other visits to Nicaragua I had not witnessed such vehement gringo-go-home sentiment. While I didn't feel threatened necessarily in the moment I was cut short. Later that day I wrote this poem, recognizing all that can sadly separate us.

Mi Corazón Lleno, Pocas Palabras Para Describir Mi Pecado

Hay una reserva en mi corazón.
Algunas veces, hay cosquillas brillantes y amarillas allí,
      también enojo monstruoso y ardiente.
Otras veces, carcajadas rosas
o gemidos grises profundos.
A veces, es donde la envidia verde y amarga reside.
Después, la caricia celeste de cariño suave y caluroso.

Y para que no se entierre más, admito dar refugio a llantos empapados
      en esta reserve. …
Hoy, es lo mejor que puedo hacer. …
Llantos para todo el sufrimiento humano, y el mío también.

Hay una reserva en mi corazón.
Por un lado, hay salud, amor y tanta belleza
      me atrevería a respirar y después perforar esta fortaleza grande que
      me abstiene de mi misma, sin fronteras, y de tí.

My Swollen Heart, Barely Words to Describe My Sin

There is a floodgate in my heart.
In moments, bright yellow tickles live there,
      monstrous crackling anger too.
At other times, deep rose-colored belly laughs
      or profound gray moans.
Sometimes, it is where bitter green envy resides.
Later, the sky-blue stroking of soft warm fondness.

And lest I bury them further, I'll admit harboring full wet sobs
      in this reservoir. …
Today it is the best I can do. …
Sobs for all human suffering, including my own.

There is a floodgate in my heart.
On one side is health, love and such beauty–
      should I dare breathe then pierce this grand fort that keeps me
      from myself, without borders, and from you.

GLOSSARY

CAPTION = THE STEPS LEADING TOWARDS MARLENE AND JOAQUÍN'S STREET

NICARAGÜENSE = NICARAGUAN
EL PRÓXIMO SALÓN PEQUEÑO = THE NEXT SMALL ROOM
LLORO AHORA = I CRY NOW
CÓRDOBAS = DENOMINATION OF NICARAGUAN MONEY
EN LAS MANOS = IN THE HANDS
DE = OF
ESCUELA = SCHOOL
COLIBRÍ = HUMMINGBIRD
RISAS = LAUGHTER

Day 7—Jinotega

VILLAGE = LA ALDEA

TIP OF THE DAY: **SAY IT A DIFFERENT WAY.**

Nosotros dimos una contribución adicional al Fondo de San Marcos de Aldea Global cuando visitamos Nicaragua.

Yesterday Marlene y yo fuimos a Jinotega to meet with the good folks at Aldea Global, a Nicaraguan social service organization, also called an NGO (non-governmental organization). Beforehand I studied the annual report they'd sent me. It was about the fund we started five years ago through my church, using a bequest designated to benefit the Nicaraguan people. Since the specific ministry project at church had folded, our priest David traveled to Nicaragua and worked with the people to further a system of microcredit. We wanted the women who are poorest to benefit. Sadly, unlike their husbands who own land, these women don't qualify to borrow funds anywhere else because they have no collateral to offer as guarantees. Through microcrédito they receive small loans plus training to develop empresitas, including small farms and closet store-fronts. Once I met the town butcher who'd learned the family trade and used her $50 loan to buy a used freezer. Because las dueñas are grouped in solidarity groups with others who then support each other, their success is assured.

Our success was practically assured too. Marlene and I met with Aldea Global's accountant and their director of training. Even though my Spanish is messy, thanks to Marlene we were able to communicate, sharing ideas and encouragement. Sometimes Marlene repeated their Spanish when I didn't understand or restated my Spanish as needed. This is a tactic we often use in preschool, "Say it a different way." At times Marlene repeated the message using fewer words or simply with her hands. She is a brilliant actress and communicator and I felt relaxed and confident by her side. I returned a casa contenta y satisfecha. And the others in our family were happy to hear our stories, complete with Marlene's beautiful, often funny descriptions and re-enactments. Es una actríz muy talentosa.

Sisterhood

By Carolina Reid

Author's Note: Remembering her travels in Nicaragua, my daughter, Carolina, had this to say.

Clarke, my brother, is my only biological sibling. However, throughout my teenage years, as I spent more time with my mother and her two sisters, Aunt Melissa and Aunt Susan, I learned what a sisterhood was. And throughout my sophomore year of college, as I cooked, lived, laughed, and cried with my four best friends from the dorms, I learned who my sisterhood was.

My first trip to Nicaragua was my mom's fourth. While we spent most of our time learning about fair trade coffee and the stories that make up every bag of beans, the experience that stuck with me the most was an afternoon we spent in an intimate circle with a dozen women who had been given loans from an organization called Aldea Global.

The basic structure of the organization is rather simple, yet wasn't picked up until the 1980s. Groups of women who have built friendships and trust between each other are given loans from investors to start their own businesses. While these businesses—convenience stores in the form of small roadside huts, handmade textiles, butchering—might seem piteous to the average American traveler, they instill a sense of pride, trust and confidence in the women who run them. Ultimately, these small business owners create a lifestyle significant enough to live a happy life and support a family. If their individual business isn't doing well, they have the support of their peers to get back on track. The group atmosphere holds each woman accountable.

In our afternoon together, each woman shared her successes because of the loan she had received from Aldea Global. Some had renewed their agreements for several years and each expressed happiness with the integrity they had witnessed and the support they had received from the organization. When I realized this sense of genuine connection in the business world was the same emotion I had felt with the gals who helped me through various ups and downs, it all made sense. The sisterhood that I knew was the same sisterhood that these women knew.

So, when I returned home with the anticipation and delight of spending another two years of school with my sisters, I also wanted to stay connected with this organization. I decided to encourage my family and friends to give money to Aldea Global in celebration of my 21st birthday.

Now, almost three years later, I manage a family-owned restaurant. I experience the same respect and support from a group of people who have a strong sense of connection. I realize that the same genuine principles of an organization like Aldea Global are applicable here at home when people trust and encourage each other co-operatively.

GLOSSARY

CAPTION = WE GAVE AN ADDITIONAL CONTRIBUTION TO ALDEA GLOBAL'S SAINT MARK'S FUND WHEN WE VISITED NICARAGUA.

MARLENE Y YO FUIMOS A JINOTEGA. = MARLENE AND I WENT TO JINOTEGA.

MICROCRÉDITO = MICROCREDIT

EMPRESITAS = SMALL BUSINESSES

LAS DUEÑAS = THE BUSINESS OWNERS

A CASA = TO HOME

CONTENTA = CONTENT

SATISFECHA = SATISFIED

ES UNA ACTRÍZ MUY TALENTOSA. = SHE IS A VERY TALENTED ACTRESS.

Day 8—Family Nest

To raise, bring up, breed, grow, nurse, nourish, fatten, create, foster = Criar

Tip of the Day: **Fall into and revel in it all.**

Yuriana con su abuela Marlene

When I arrived in Matagalpa, I was surprised and pleased to find that Yuriana, 7 months, and Diego, 3 months, are now part of Marlene and Joaquín's family. They are strikingly gorgeous babies, as babies are. As the one school psychologist in my school district who works with los más pequeños y sus padres, I know a lot about early child development. I know these children are being raised well. They are content, alert and curious. They cry when they are hungry and fuss (a very little bit) when they are tired. I know because they live on either side of my room and my windows are often open.

The babies live with seven others in the extended family: abuelos, madres, un padre, y hermanos. And while Yuriana's father, Yuri, lives on his nearby farm, he visits often. Los bebés are always in someone's brazos; they are passed from one to another—uno por uno. They seem happy and infinitely well-cared for. Sometimes, I'll admit, my concern for her fine motor development peaks because she rarely plays with toys or explores with her mouth. Or I wonder what happens when he skips crawling, which appears to usually be the case because he will rarely be on the floor.

Nevertheless I know the most important thing at this age is that children are attached to a caregiver and feel safe. And I see the beautiful examples of Madelin, 13, and Fernando, 9, the other two children in this household who are bright, social and happy. Yuriana shows a healthy, curious interest in me but at the same time, shies away just as she should at this age—after all I am a stranger who has come into her nido. The other night when she was admittedly tired I took her from Marlene and bounced her on my knee. She was interested for a few seconds but quickly fussed and Marlene scooped her right back.

I am living this same experience. This family has welcomed me with open arms into this broad and deep nido at the top of a hill. They are collectively committed to my safety and happiness, bienestar first and then to me learning Spanish. I have this comfortable espacio privado to myself and I can close or open the door as I like. I can join the family in el salón or la cocina or retreat depending on my mood and needs. I am beginning to venture onto the patio y jardín. And I notice that there is always someone nearby to chat with me as much or as little as I like, explain a word or concept and to gently correct my mistakes in the moment. I am seamlessly passed from one to another with infinite patience and care. Yet again, I feel exceedingly agradecida.

The more I learn, the more I recognize the difficulty of this task I have chosen—this path to learning Spanish. In some ways it is a natural and common process. Toddlers do it all the time, going on to learn two or three languages, without accents, before puberty. Just as raising a child is the most common practice in the world, to do it well, it takes a village. I am witnessing this very phenomenon, up close and personal. And I cannot imagine a better way to criar my Spanish development. It can only improve and flourish in a nourishing environment like this one. Little by little, from one gentle teacher to another, I will revel in the creation of mi segunda lengua.

GLOSSARY

CAPTION = YURIANA WITH HER GRANDMOTHER MARLENE

LOS MÁS PEQUEÑOS = THE YOUNGEST

SUS PADRES = THEIR PARENTS

ABUELOS = GRANDPARENTS

MADRES = MOTHERS

PADRE = FATHER

HERMANOS = BROTHERS AND SISTERS

LOS BEBÉS = BABIES

BRAZOS = ARMS

UNO POR UNO = ONE BY ONE

NIDO = NEST

BIENESTAR = WELL-BEING

ESPACIO PRIVADO = PRIVATE SPACE

EL SALÓN = LIVING ROOM

LA COCINA = KITCHEN

JARDÍN = GARDEN

AGRADECIDA = GRATEFUL

SEGUNDA LENGUA = SECOND LANGUAGE

LA FAMILIA = THE FAMILY

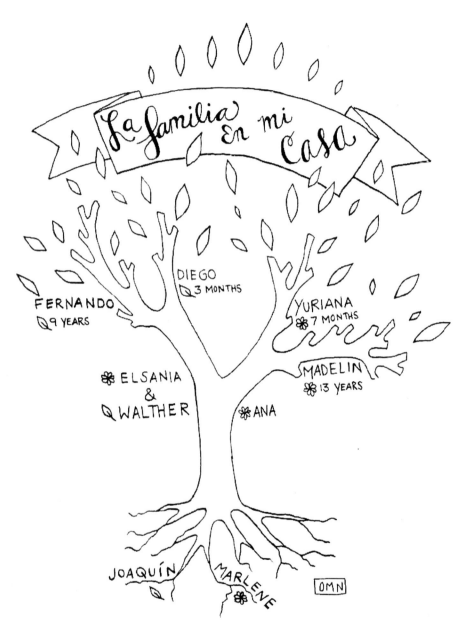

Illustrated by Ollie Mae Nicoll

Day 9—At Yuri's Farm

Petronila trató de ensañarme a hacer tortillas en el fogon de leña.

You know the expression: I feel as if I have died and estoy en el cielo. I am here at Yuri's finca con mi familia nicaragüese. And it is bliss. Primero, ayer, we went on a brief tour of the farm. Yuri showed me the beneficio húmedo. We walked amongst the parakeets and mariposas and talked with the workers. The cows and chickens are just across the tiny road from nuestra casa—un edificio for cooking and one for sleeping. I am perched on the patio in between the buildings with a pot of very fresh coffee con mis libros y diccionario. I slept solidly more than eight hours. They even promise me there is hot water for a shower later. La bebé is cooing. Literally her sounds of contentment are like those of una paloma and are como música para mí. Me gustan mucho. Todo está bien, muy bien. This is Sabbath.

Prayer

Author's Note: During our first Saint Mark's tour in Nicaragua, I wrote this simple prayer while in the coffee co-operative of La Pita, Nicaragua.

Querida Madre, Fuego Santo en mí—
Tu puedes mostrarme como.
Tu voluntad sola, si tú quieres, si tú quieres.
Muchisimas gracias,
Amén

Dear Mother, Holy Fire in me—
You can show me how.
Your will only, if you wish, if you wish.
With much gratitude,
Amen

GLOSSARY

CAPTION = PETRONILA TRIED TO TEACH ME TO MAKE TORTILLAS OVER THE OPEN FIRE.

FINCA = FARM
PRIMERO = FIRST
AYER = YESTERDAY
BENEFICIO HUMÉDO = WET MILL
NUESTRA = OUR
UN EDIFICIO = A BUILDING
MIS LIBROS = MY BOOKS
DICCIONARIO = DICTIONARY
PALOMA = DOVE
COMO MÚSICA PARA MI = LIKE MUSIC TO ME
ME GUSTAN MUCHO. = I LIKE THEM A LOT.
TODO ESTÁ BIEN, MUY BIEN. = ALL IS WELL, VERY WELL.

Day 10—Returning to Town

BUS = EL AUTOBÚS

TIP OF THE DAY: **RIDE IT.**

Los taxis en Matagalpa se comparten y se llenan también, como los autobuses.

More than once in an airport my daughter Carolina has reminded me, "You're in the river now, Mom, just ride it." Early yesterday morning, I channeled her words. First a las cinco y otra vez a las seis, I realized that I had not precisely understood all of our discussion the night before about our wake-up, breakfast and bus times for the next morning. Understated, my Spanish is not precise yet. Part of the joint discussion amongst the four of us women in our bunk room como una fiesta de pijamas was about what time we'd need to get up to accommodate everyone in the bathroom. I set my alarm for 4:45, which as it turned out was the correct agreed-upon time. Madelin's alarm sounded first, sassy and admittedly a bit jarring at that hour, and my light chimes followed a minute later.

With our bathing complete, including both muchachas washing their long beautiful locks, we wolfed down our last exceedingly fresh and delicious breakfast at the hands of Petronila. She had already arrived before the crack of dawn to start her workweek. Before leaving her kitchen, I folded my lacey hot pink headband into su mano with a sincere thank you for showing me how to make tortillas over an open fire the night before. Even though my head is about twice the size of Petronila's, I can imagine her beauty as the headband sits upon her dark black pelo. Or more likely, that of one of her nietas who will receive the circulating gift from her abuela.

After a last trek up the hill we arrived at the store and bus stop with 45 minutes to spare. Now I understood why Yuri had said, "Tranquila, Penélope, tranquila," when I had assumed my customary norteamericana rush. Instead I found myself again in Nicaragua, hurrying up to wait. And for the second morning in a row, I watched the hot and dark pink puesta del sol. Everything was washed with a spectacular glow of bienestar. Earlier in the week I had seen this phenomenon when returning from Jinotega but on the other side of the day—God's regular and obvious blessing of first el día before us and then la noche to come. I am reminded as I write that there are often sweet kisses like these that I miss when I stop breathing in the moment. Instead, I want to quietly notice the absolute goodness as these days of mi aventura nicaragüense unfold.

But back to el autobús … one of mis deseos for this trip was to ride the public bus. I had scared myself about being in a crowd of Nicaraguans who only speak Spanish; I wanted to address this fear by traveling as the locals do. Now I certainly have met this fear head on. The first bus on Monday morning was una experiencia sin precio, slowly covering the mountainous direct roads from the comunidad of La Florida back to Matagalpa. Con buena suerte, Marlene y yo got the first seat on the bus beside the front door. I could witness every person—bebé, toddler, viejo, trabajadora—who entered and packed every conceivable space around us. At one point I counted nine people, including a tiny peaceful newborn in her mother's arms, crowding the space in front of us around the driver and on the steps leading to the always open entry door of the bus. From my vantage point, I could see our up-and-down course, cross myself and pray for good brakes and steady driving as needed. During our time together, I watched the very capable son of the driver hop on and off the bus to welcome travelers and help them add tires, bags of coffee and rice, construction materials and other goods to the top of our bus. I didn't see live chickens arrive but Marlene explained that they were likely there amongst us.

I was glad to arrive safely on the bustling streets of my host city and to walk the four uphill blocks to nuestra casa and the welcoming arms of Joaquín y Elsania. It was 8:20 a.m. and I had already lived an experience of a lifetime in 90 minutes traveling a mere 16 kilómetros.

Poor People?

While Nicaragua has been described as the second poorest nation in the Western Hemisphere, because I chose to immerse myself in the beautiful song that is Spanish, I stumbled on one golden and exceedingly rich opportunity after another during my second visit to this small but powerful country during the summer of 2011. For instance, I saw the teenage girls in my family dance before local mayors, national representatives and 300 interested citizens at a forum on clean potable water.

I heard one of today's leading Nicaraguan women revolutionaries, Katia Cardenal, sing en vivo on my first night in Nicaragua while Noelia's brother plied me with Toñas. I witnessed a medical clinic at La Sombra to which 300 campesinas came for very basic care, some walking several miles to attend and all wearing their Sunday-best clothes. I played games with the pregnant women at Casa Maderna, the preschoolers in the Sunday School class in San Ramón as well as with children at the lodges and in my Matagalpa home.

I watched "Cuna de Gato," a telenovela each night with Marlene and Joaquín, in between drop-in visits to their home from sellers of fresh bread and lingerie. I visited three schools—urban and rural, two primary and one secondary—and spoke with principals, teachers and students plus learned how children with special needs are served. I asked people what they remembered about the long war that led to revolution and ousted the 40-year Somoza dictatorship. They answered directly in their language about piles of dead bodies in the streets and about their grandparents feeding revolutionaries quietly at midnight on the family farm in the mountains.

These are not poor people; rather Nicaragua is an impoverished country. More than 50% are un- or underemployed and many are hungry, living without clean water to drink, without plumbing, without regular health and dental care. While public education is available, uniforms are encouraged which poses a hardship for many families. Plus there is often no transportation available to and from school, and the hours for study are short, either 7:30 a.m.-noon or 12:30 p.m.-5:00 p.m.

Still, the government and her citizens are choosing to preserve and honor one of their most important resources: the natural tropical environment which varies greatly—two coasts, mountains, beaches, large lakes, volcanoes and islands. On this my second trip I chose to soak it up, walking lots every day, visiting the mountains and Ometepe Island complete with river kayaking and siting Cayman alligators, iguanas, butterflies and birds galore.

I witnessed conservation at the most basic level: taking cold showers (which were actually welcome in the humidity), washing dishes in a soaking sink and not flushing as often. When Rob arrived, we splurged. Besides staying at La Sombra in the mountains, we stayed a few nights at a luxury lodge on Ometepe Island not unlike what I imagine resorts are like in the South Pacific—individual cabins, flowers everywhere, fresh-squeezed tamarind juice upon arrival, hot showers—all completely off the electrical grid thanks to solar panels.

In this country everyone shares what they have including rooms, beds and walls. Efficiency is built in. Clearly I have much to learn here.

GLOSSARY

CAPTION = THE TAXIS EN MATAGALPA ARE SHARED AND FULL TOO, JUST LIKE THE BUSES.

A LAS CINCO Y OTRA VEZ A LAS SEIS = AT FIVE O'CLOCK AND AGAIN AT SIX O'CLOCK

COMO UNA FIESTA DE PIJAMAS = LIKE A PAJAMA PARTY

MUCHACHAS = YOUNG WOMEN

SU MANO = HER HAND

PELO = HAIR

NIETAS = GRANDDAUGHTERS

ABUELA = GRANDMOTHER

NORTEAMERICANA = NORTH AMERICAN

LA PUESTA DEL SOL = SUNSET

EL DÍA = THE DAY

LA NOCHE = THE NIGHT

MI AVENTURA = MY ADVENTURE

MIS DESEOS = MY DESIRES

UNA EXPERIENCIA SIN PRECIO = A PRICELESS EXPERIENCE

CON BUENA SUERTE = LUCKILY

COMUNIDAD = COMMUNITY

Y YO = AND I

VIEJO = OLD MAN

TRABAJADORA = WORKER

KILÓMETROS = KILOMETERS

EN VIVO = LIVE

TOÑA = NICARAGUAN BEER

CAMPESINOS = THOSE WHO LIVE AND WORK OFF THE LAND IN THE COUNTRYSIDE

CUNA DE GATO = CAT'S CRADLE

TELENOVELA = SOAP OPERA

Day 11—With my American Friends

Mis amigos, Richard Robohm y Lynn Edwards viven en Matagalpa. Hace 25 años, Lynn y yo fuimos vecinas en las casas flotantes de Seattle. La cena en su casa estuvo muy rica y especial.

I am very curious about why the coincidences pile up for me when I'm in Nicaragua. I suspect that this way of living, of awareness and goodness and noticing, is available to me all the time including at home in los EEUU (los Estados Unidos de América … also abbreviated EUA in Spanish but not as often).

Maybe I just take my time here, or move more deliberately, or feel vulnerable therefore am more careful or grateful when things unfold well— which is usually my experience. Five years ago, after my initial tour in

Nicaragua, we arranged an intercambio speaking tour for social entrepreneur friend Noelia Corrales in Seattle. After she returned home, Noelia asked me to tell a certain Lynn Edwards (who also lived in Seattle) about Matagalpa. Like me, Lynn had traveled with a tour group to Nicaragua, would retire soon and was interested in relocating somewhere en el país. My first question was whether or not this Lynn Edwards could possibly be the same person I'd lived alongside on a houseboat muelle in downtown Seattle 25 years ago? Amazingly Lynn was my former vecina.

Last night, a quarter of a century later, I joined Lynn and her esposo, Richard, for a fabulous dinner of passion fruit daiquiris and Niçoise salad in their beautifully restored and remodeled home on the flanks of Cerro Apante just outside of Matagalpa. While the food was delicious, the conversation in English was even better, nothing less than manna from heaven.

Later though, I felt the reality of choosing to live such a special time— Advent and Christmas—away from my own beloved family members. Occasionally I have connected via Wi-Fi and seen rolling Facebook photos and commentary as the Nativity season back home unfolds and peaks. I found myself actually tearing up a wee bit on the street when I recognized someone who reminded me his name is Wilcón (a name from the Atlantic coast, one that originated from the Creole/English word "Welcome"). Wilcón told me he now resides in Athens, Georgia where he studies technical science. I remembered that in the past he had been a teacher at mi escuela. When he told me he's considering moving back to Matagalpa because he doesn't want to be un extranjero any more, my eyes watered and I felt tan solitaria. It was such a breath of fresh air to be able to converse especially given the bittersweet understanding of homesickness we shared.

Alas, I work in the schools. Although there is a definite advantage to having free time during the holidays, I'll admit the draw of retirement. Then I'll be able to travel when kids are in school and I can stay home for Christmas.

Socio-Cultural Tourism in Nicaragua
with Noelia Corrales

Author's Note: The paragraph that follows was used in a flyer to describe Noelia Corrales and encourage people to attend presentations during her speaking tour in Seattle.

"Noelia Corrales is a social entrepreneur and co-founder of Matagalpa Tours, an organization that promotes socio-cultural tourism, environmental sustainability and women's empowerment in the rural mountains of northern Nicaragua. She is committed to providing work and leadership opportunities to people in her community in order to fight the pressure of migration. She also speaks to a variety of audiences about the importance of fair trade, human rights, social justice, environmental education and economic sustainability."

GLOSSARY

CAPTION = MY FRIENDS, RICHARD ROBOHM AND LYNN EDWARDS LIVE IN MATAGALPA. TWENTY-FIVE YEARS AGO, LYNN AND I WERE NEIGHBORS ON THE HOUSEBOATS IN SEATTLE. DINNER AT THEIR HOUSE WAS VERY DELICIOUS AND SPECIAL.

LOS ESTADOS UNIDOS DE AMÉRICA = UNITED STATES OF AMERICA
INTERCAMBIO = EXCHANGE
EN EL PAÍS = IN THE COUNTRY
MUELLE = DOCK
VECINA = NEIGHBOR
ESPOSO = HUSBAND
TAN SOLITARIA = SO LONELY

Day 12—Christmas Cookies

Hicimos galletas de Navidad con la receta de mi madre.

Anoche we made cookies. The children were beside themselves with glee and anticipation, especially 9-year-old Fernando. And so was I. Even though my sloppy Spanish is still barely understandable, this niño simpático will finally talk to me and even with me. His high pre-pubescent voz is easily amongst mis favoritas aquí.

I had brought along cookie cutters, sugar sprinkles and a card with my mother's family receta for sugar cookies. Early in my visit I gave these items plus an oven thermometer to Marlene for her cumpleaños earlier in the month. Few ovens come with built-in thermometers in Nicaraguan homes and I'd been told this was a coveted item.

In my culture, we make Christmas cookies and celebrate with parties all month long. That's not so here. While there has been a Christmas tree in el salón since I arrived, its lights are never on and I only noticed small presents starting to collect under it yesterday.

I gave Marlene the cookie supplies soon after I arrived. She and everyone else seemed delighted with the gift. Together we decided what ingredients might be missing from the household and the next day I picked up mantequilla, powdered sugar and baking powder. When I delivered these to her, thinking this might be a fun activity for early in my visit, she stashed the foodstuffs away saying, I think, that if we made them right away, they'd all be gone by Nochebuena.

So last night was our adventure in baking. Marlene was demasiado cansada after a full day of chores—cooking for all of us, doing the weekly cleaning of my room (including a change of sheets and the addition of a quilt) and caring for Yuriana who chose this day to skip her nap. So Joaquín was our helper when Marlene slipped out apparently for a little extra shopping. We started the process late and had to wait an hour while the dough chilled. Fortunately, Fernando was granted an extension of his bedtime and we gathered around the table at 8:30 p.m. to roll out the dough, cut it and decorate.

I noticed how very little vocabulary I have for this task and plan to ask Diana for help during class. The kids must have seen the process completed on TV because once we figured out an acceptable glass to use as our rolling pin and located the spatula, they were off and running. Marlene had pulled out two giant turkey basting pans for us to use as cookie sheets. And Joaquín was available to light the gas oven immediately before baking. There's no wasteful pre-heating in the tropics, one of many eco-conscious and economical methods typical in Nicaragua.

I think I might have inadvertently transferred the cookies to a treasured glass plato at the very end of the process instead of bothering Marlene by asking what to use. For this, she seemed a bit annoyed and asked several questions about where I had found this plate. Quisiera to try to share my assumptions and limited understanding about this with her later*. Still all in all, it was another grand aventura con esta buena familia. As such Nochebuena begins and en mi corazón, I am ready to celebrate la familia preciosa de Jesús.

*Marlene had actually misplaced this special plate and wanted to figure out how it was lost and where I found it.

Environmental Sustainability

From Noelia Corrales

Author's Note: After visiting us for the speaking tour and then spending time with cousins in California, Noelia Corrales sent a long letter expressing her appreciation and reflecting on what she had seen and learned. Here is the segment containing her ponderings about environmental sustainability:

"Sometimes I heard comments from people in Seattle showing a strong need to have things of value, such as large TVs, luxury cars, beautiful houses. The same was true of my family in California. I watched their faces at the mall wanting to buy everything they really do not need and their desire to give me material gifts, and the anger on their faces when I told them no. It seems so unfair, the social construct of the patriarchal-capitalist system of measuring life by what I have rather than what I am, wanting more and not valuing who we are as people. And it seems even more unfair that we let ourselves get carried away by that system and we accept it as a part of life, while it denies us the essence of love and the source of being.

I was shocked by the indiscriminate use of disposable material to eat and drink, much more in California, and I am concerned when I hear responses like the one a cousin gave me. When I suggested she avoid drinking water from plastic bottles, she replied, 'Don't worry, here the gringos recycle all the plastic.' She seemed convinced that recycling is the medicine for environmental pollution. That scares me. It scares me that recycling could become a justification for consumption, for waste, and for the lack of concern for the damage caused by the garbage we produce. I once heard that if everyone in the world wanted to live the way people live in the United States, we would need seven more planets to meet all the human 'needs.' Now, after my trip, I understand better what they meant."

GLOSSARY

CAPTION = WE MADE CHRISTMAS COOKIES WITH MY MOTHER'S RECIPE.

ANOCHE = LAST NIGHT
NIÑO SIMPÁTICO = NICE BOY
VOZ = VOICE
MI FAVORITO = MY FAVORITE
AQUÍ = HERE
RECETA = RECIPE
CUMPLEAÑOS = BIRTHDAY
EL NACIMIENTO = CRÈCHE
MANTEQUILLA = BUTTER
DEMASIADO CANSADA = TOO TIRED
PLATO = PLATE
QUISIERA = I WOULD LIKE TO
ESTA BUENA FAMILIA = THIS GOOD FAMILY
EN MI CORAZÓN = IN MY HEART
LA FAMILIA PRECIOSA = THE PRECIOUS FAMILY

Day 13—A Quiet Holiday

CHRISTMAS = NAVIDAD

TIP OF THE DAY: **LISTEN.**

El nacimiento en el parque central de Matagalpa

I would be remiss if I didn't write about el montón de sonidos y ruidos around me all the time here in Matagalpa. It was especially nice at the farm and also here on the patio where I can notice sounds of nature such as the steady breeze in the bushes and birds chirping constantly including gentle palomas cooing along with the riotous gallo. Barking dogs are a frequent addition to the cacophony too. And there is music from all sides—on the other side of the wall we share with a neighbor; farther away from loud speakers perched on top of un coche that circulates through the city with cheer de Navidad and advertisements; and the chimes of some vendor or another announcing an opportunity to buy pan o helado o even lingerie using catalogs brought into the home for easy shopping. The TV is blaring from our living room nearby. Motorcycles are revving and a car is backfiring in the street.

Still I'm certain any Matagalpino would say it is quiet here this morning. We are on the other side of una gran fiesta that started in the late afternoon yesterday and only began to settle down a little bit when I crashed around 3 a.m. I especially noticed the cathedral bells sounding fervently every half hour in the late afternoon before la misa began at dusk. And then at midnight bottle rockets, fireworks and firecrackers exploded for an hour or so, tapering off slightly as the wee hours grew.

This constant ruckus is a cultural difference I am trying to make peace with somehow. My favorite sounds last night, of course, were the music of the Spanish language all around me, especially as I noticed that I understand more and more of it, por lo menos the theme of almost all discussions and more and more often, the nuances too. I have decided that when there is deep constant laughter, or tears for that matter, I will join in. I don't need to know the whole story and I acknowledge that sometimes it's about me. I notice that the conversation slows or stops less and less often as I throw in a comment or two and that Marlene shows off our friendship as we stroll arm-in-arm up the street to stop in at a nearby cousin's casa. There we hear Marlene's sister re-tell the Christ Child's birth story yet again to rolled eyes and, often, pursed and quivering lips that are a Nicaraguan means of expression. I can only assume the teenagers are tired of the same story told again and again but, most likely out of respect for the elder aunt (or perhaps for the ancient story itself?) everyone listens half-heartedly.

When the light of a new dawn has come, and the party animal in me has lived to tell the story another day, espero there is another trip to the countryside in my future this weekend. I suspect the relative quiet of a farm or a coffee co-operative would be saludable for me. I have a slight cough and am reminding myself to drink water constantly, take my pro-biotics and multi-vitamins, listen to my meditation tapes, wash my hands and get massages regularly. Tomorrow is the day I need to start malaria medication in preparation for the coast. We'll see what I decide. One of the reasons I chose to travel now during the dry season is that there are hardly any mosquitoes. What's best? Vamos a ver.

Duérmete, Mi Niña

Author's Note: Marlene sang this beautiful lullaby to Yuriana as she rocked her. Christmas Day was the first day I listened for the words and wrote them down.

Duérmete, Mi Niña

Duérmete mi niña, duérmete mi amor

Duérmete pedazo de mi corazón.

(Cantando en voz baja)

Sleep, My Girl

Sleep my girl, sleep my love,

Sleep a piece of my heart.

(Singing in a quiet voice)

GLOSSARY

CAPTION = THE CRÈCHE IN MATAGALPA'S CENTRAL PARK.

EL MONTÓN = A HEAP
DE SONIDOS Y RUIDOS = OF SOUNDS AND NOISES
GALLO = ROOSTER
UN COCHE = A CAR
PAN = BREAD
HELADO = ICE CREAM
UNA GRAN FIESTA = ONE BIG PARTY
POR LO MENOS = AT LEAST
ESPERO = I HOPE
SALUDABLE = HEALTHY
VAMOS A VER. = WE'LL SEE.

Day 14—Boxing Day

POETRY = LA POESÍA

TIP OF THE DAY: **JUST BREATHE.**

Descansando después de las fiestas en el patio de Marlene.

Coral de los poetas del alba

Por: Pablo Antonio Cuadra

¡Resurrexit sicut dixit Alleluia!

¡Ah! ¡Ya empezó el mundo a dar su vuelta!

Los cuatro vientos han hecho girar los perfumes que reposaban.

El perfume de la luna se ha derramado en las ubres,

en los pechos de la mujer se ha derramado.

El perfume de la estrella solitaria se ha movido en las rosas,

en los labios de las doncellas ha sonreído.

El perfume del silencio ha recorrido la palabra,

en la voz de los poetas ha florecido.

Ved a los hombres que piden sus caballos,

los hombres que dan voces en las sábanas del alba.

¡Ah! ya fueron formados los caballos y los caminos nuevos.

Todos los animales, todos los elementos han encontrado su novedad.

Esta es la hora en que reconocemos la infancia del niñito,

esta es la hora de la ternura del ternero.

La hora que está balando, cantando, accurrucando.

Ya llegaron las mujeres, las madrugadoras, al nido de los ángeles.

Ya regresan las mujeres, las madrugadoras,

     con los rostros recién lavados,

con las gotas de la mañana en el nacimiento de sus cabellos.

El cielo—han dicho—es el dulce país de la luz.

Los hombres han montado sus caballos y se encaminan a su edad.

Van por sus años andando.

Vamos con la luz a la cintura, vamos chapoteando.

Nosotros sabemos que la felicidad es una suma de auroras.

Hemos bebido el vino de la mañana,

en los corrales, en los establos hemos bebido el jugo del alba.

¡Somos los hombres nuevos!

Chorale of the Poets of the Dawn

By: Pablo Antonio Cuadra
English Translation: Sarah Hornsby and Matthew C. Hornsby

Resurrexit sicut dixit Alleluia!

Ah! Now the world has begun to turn!

The four winds have made swirl the perfumes that reposed.

The perfume of the moon has been spilled on the udders,

on the breasts of woman it has been spilled.

The perfume of the solitary star has moved in the roses,

on the lips of the maidens it has smiled.

The perfume of silence has surveyed the word,

on the voice of poets it has flowered.

Go to the men who ask for their horses,

the men who give voice in the sheets of the dawn.

Ah! the horses were just formed and the new paths.

All the animals, all the elements have encountered their newness.

This is the hour we recognize the infancy of the little boy,

this is the hour of the tenderness of the calf.

The hour that is bleating, singing, huddling.

The women just arrived, the early risers, to the nest of the angels.

The women now return, the early risers, with freshly washed faces,

with the drops of the morning on the birth of their hair.

Heaven—they have said—is the sweet country of light.

Men have mounted their horses and they set out to their age.

They spend their years on the move.

We go with the light up to our waist, we go splashing.

We know that happiness is a sum of auroras.

We have drunk the wine of the morning,

in the corrals, in the stables we have drunk the juice of the dawn.

We are the new men!

Happy Christmas!
From Diana Iris Huerrera Castro

Author's Note: One of my favorite Christmas gifts was a card from my teacher, Diana, made on hand-crafted recycled stationary.

> Querida Penny…   23 dic. 2014.
>   Quiero desearte una feliz
> navidad, llena de amor, de
> milagros y alegrías.
>   Espero que este 2015 esté
> lleno de prosperidad.
> ¡Feliz Navidad y Próspero
> Año Nuevo!
>   att: Diana

December 23, 2014

Dear Penny …

I wish you a happy Christmas, full of love, of miracles and happiness.

I hope that this 2015 is full of prosperity.

Happy Christmas and Prosperous New Year!

From Diana

GLOSSARY

CAPTION = RESTING ON MARLENE'S PATIO AFTER THE PARTIES

Day 15—Sick

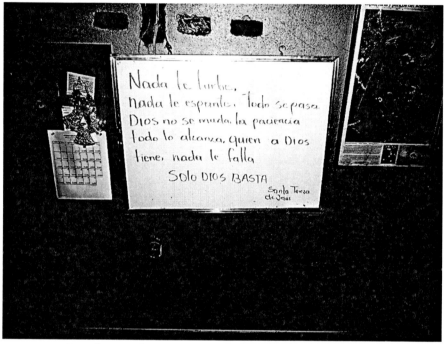

Desafortunadamente estuve enferma antes de las fiestas.

There is a lovely chant that encapsulates the words of Julian of Norwich:

All shall be well

And all shall be well

And all manner of things shall be well

Be well.

At least I live with this certainty. Even though I have una gripe with my usual symptoms of a runny nose and una tos fea, in some relatively farther-away-than-usual corner of my mind and heart I know that All. Is. Well.

And I found a similar quote by Saint Teresa on a white board at la escuela, "Nada te turbe."

In Spanish there is a word for this: esperanza/esparar/esperazada. Maybe you know this phenomenon as hope, to hope, hopeful. As I have come to embrace Spanish, I am learning the breadth and depth of this word because it also means to wait for and simultaneously to expect. It can bear a certainty about goodness that embodies deep faith to me.

Interestingly these people who speak Spanish also have verb tenses called "The Subjunctive." Espero my first introduction to the tense next week. Several years ago, when Rob, Carolina and I spent a week together immersed and studying Spanish, Rob and I were placed in the Advanced Beginner class and Carolina in the next level up. Among other things, she studied the subjunctive tense. I remember the conversations over almuerzo when Carolina described this idea that people who speak Spanish fluently, talk about the future in a tentative way using subjunctive tenses. Clearly this way of speaking about what might occur beyond the present moment is not nearly as presumptive as life is in my American culture and there is a way of speaking that describes this. Instead of saying, "Next week, I'll hear an introduction to the subjunctive," it's a bit like, "La semana próxima, God willing, I'll hear an introduction to the subjunctive."

"Espero" fits well here: I hope, I expect, I wait for. In this very moment, espero méjorarme. Truthfully, también espero la muerte de mi papá. Tiene 94 años. Usa oxígeno todo el tiempo pero ahora está bendecido pues todavía tiene su mente y tenemos a mi mamá, su mejor enfermera. Pero, morirá. Quízas, mientras estoy en Nicaragua. ¿Quién sabe? Espero con un corazón triste y agobiado. Es posible que por esto tenga este resfriado tan malo.

From Here Inside God, Merry Christmas!

Author's Note: Two years ago, my children were both traveling separately in South America and met on Christmas Day. My elderly parents were staying with us for the holidays. My father was recovering from a fall while playing ping pong and my mother was his best nurse as always. Here's what I wrote while sitting in our living room at home.

The three who are older than me in this living room are snoozing. So is the one being who is younger, my dog. I am still and quiet, through and through, and am sitting here inside God, listening to the sounds of Her breathing. It is as if the clock ticking nearby is God's heart and the whir of the dishwasher is His intestines, finishing the cleaning after the second feast "with company" in 24 hours. I use quotes because this Christmastime, I am throwing my definitions of company, and family too, wide open.

I cannot be more grateful that I have elderly parents who are here and well. They are giving me a fresh understanding of the kind of healing that is possible at 92 and the joy that comes from deeply caring at 84. I started the day with 30 blissful seconds of beaming before speaking, seeing Clarke's and Carolina's laughing faces Skyped in from far away. They had found each other after traveling on Christmas Eve via bus and plane to convene in downtown Buenos Aires on Christmas morn. I am grateful to have young adult children who know what a gift it is, most of all, to trade stories in person with a sibling who speaks your very first language fluently. And I have my sisters who have entertained me all day long with blog posts, e-cards, and Facebook statuses about what Modern Family is.

Plus, there are my friends, such very dear ones, who have come to make cookies, sip eggnog and break bread with me, worried that I might be too sad here on the first Christmas away from my kids in 25 years, only to find that I am living inside God, absolutely enveloped, and so are they. Whatever words we use to try to describe this Grand Mystery, we trade the same oxygen cells, hear the same carols from the stereo and sense the pulse of the Other Beings alongside us that is palpable even across miles and continents.

GLOSSARY

CAPTION = UNFORTUNATELY I WAS SICK AFTER THE FESTIVITIES.

UNA GRIPE = THE FLU
UNA TOS FEA = AN UGLY COUGH
NADA TE TURBE = MAY NOTHING DISTURB YOU
ALMUERZO = LUNCH
LA SEMANA PRÓXIMA = NEXT WEEK

TAMBIÉN ESPERO LA MUERTE DE MI PAPÁ. TIENE 94 AÑOS. USA OXÍGENO TODO EL TIEMPO PERO AHORA ESTÁ BENDECIDO PUES TODAVÍA TIENE SU MENTE Y TENEMOS A MI MAMÁ, SU MEJOR ENFERMERA. PERO, MORIRÁ. QUÍZAS, MIENTRAS ESTOY EN NICARAGUA. ¿QUIÉN SABE? ESPERO CON UN CORAZÓN TRISTE Y AGOBIADO. ES POSIBLE QUE POR ESTO TENGA ESTE RESFRIADO TAN MALO. = I ALSO WAIT FOR THE DEATH OF MY DAD. HE IS 94. HE USES OXYGEN ALL THE TIME NOW. HE IS BLESSED TO STILL HAVE HIS MIND AND WE HAVE MY MOM WHO IS HIS BEST NURSE. BUT HE WILL DIE. PERHAPS WHILE I AM IN NICARAGUA, WHO KNOWS? I WAIT WITH A SAD AND HEAVY HEART. IT'S POSSIBLE THIS IS WHY I HAVE SUCH A BAD COLD.

Day 16—Sunday at Home

A MIXTURE = UNA MEZCLA

TIP OF THE DAY: **NOTICE AND REFLECT.**

La perra Fiona proteje la casa mientras Marlene ayuda a Fernando con su bici.

It is domingo. Fernando has joined me on the patio with his brand new bicicleta de su abuela para Navidad. He is practicing braking con sus manos. Back and forth, back and forth, in this 25-foot space. I am remembering my favorite Christmas present ever when my sisters and I found brand new bicis de Schwinn in front of the Christmas tree from Santa Claus. It was a complete surprise then but it is not astonishing now to witness Fernando's delight as he gathers confidence and skill. Unexpected for me is mi mismo deleite as I watch and even offer my bits of consejo, "Estas listo con tus manos? Mejor frena con tus manos, no con tus zapatos."

My host sobrino is flashing his new watch around the patio as he moves and is calling the reflection that is jumping around una mariposa. And milagro de los milagros, I am understanding him. Next, he has told me the story of his favorite dog, a Husky named Lulu.

My initial thought today was that I'd write about all the little cultural differences that I don't want to forget. After all, it is Sunday and I feel safe and grounded here. Tranquila; nada me turba. I had this silly idea that if I stayed home I would waste a day in the tropics but then I woke up and learned that Marlene was sick too. And I gave myself permission to just rest, write, read, and visit with the family—like Rob and I do at the beach. I have found the perfect perch beside the front gate where there is mixed shade and sun. And I can even pick up Wi-Fi occasionally from tía Lylian's next door. On Christmas Day, I Skyped with Rob and Carolina at Lylian's house and now I have la llave for use nearby. I am amazed to feel, again, thoroughly content while I visit with folks as they come and go. And I am reminded of my grandfather who sat beside our front door in his old age, willing to watch us come and go and enjoy a bit of conversation con cada uno.

Clearly this day is unfolding en el ritmo de la familia. I started the day sick and was determined to stay in mis pijamas as long as possible. Slowly I have been changing to street clothes, first adding pants, then a bra. Later I took off the socks under my sandals as the day warmed. And now, hours later I am completely dressed and it is just before noon. Still en realidad, mi ropa today is very pajama-like y una mezcla of light and dark, sol y sombra.

From my perch I can see la perra, Fiona. She is tethered most of the time en el jardín on a very short leash. The first time I came to Nicaragua I learned during our orientation with Witness for Peace that animals usually serve another function here besides solely being pets. Cats rid the home of rodents. Dogs protect the household with their barking announcements that someone new has arrived or their growls and bites to defend the property and inhabitants. I remember my very first night in a modest home with a family in Managua. I got up in the middle of the dark night to use the one communal toilet and the dog went nuts. It was all I could do to draw up my courage, calm her and do my business. The second night in this home I noticed that this dog recognized my smell and voice and didn't bark, leaving me free to notice the sky full of stars from the open-air patio through which I passed to reach el baño.

En la casa de Marlene, I have noticed my judgments about the way los perros, Fiona and Dodi, live. From what I can tell they are tied up almost all of the time and have a very small space to sniff and scratch and move. Still, I know that others in Fiona's litter tienen bastante suerte to live at Yuri's finca. Of her litter, some were sold including Fernando's favorite, Lulu, adding to the family's resources. Fiona's presence here has given me the chance to add to mi vocabulario: ladrar and correa, for example. I have learned that my dog Roxy is una Labrador pura. Fiona has eyes like mine: celeste. She is the breed of la mascota de mi universidad—a Washington Husky. Todo es una mezcla hermosa de memorias e historias ahora para mi y otra oportunidad para praticar los usos de por y para, tarea de mis clases de español.

Even Dogs Die

I miss our yellow lab, Roxy. She broke her ACL about a year before she died. She didn't slow down much before then. Even though she'd weathered mast cell disease (dog cancer) when she was 5, she returned to fetching and swimming and following us around with a vengeance. You know what they say about dogs—they love you unconditionally—but you have to experience it to believe it in your bones.

In her youth, Roxy would wait behind our glass door for me to return from work. And when she saw me she'd leap, all four paws off the floor at the same time levitating about three feet off the ground. If that ain't enthusiasm, what is? She was almost 13 years old when I left for Nicaragua and was still going strong. She and Rob were good company for each other during those short, cold days and long, dark nights in the Northwest around Christmastime.

Sky

Jumper

to Penny from her Dad
Happy Birthday

Illustrated by John R. Clarke

GLOSSARY

CAPTION = THE DOG, FIONA, PROTECTS THE HOME WHILE MARLENE HELPS FERNANDO WITH HIS BIKE.

DOMINGO = SUNDAY
BICICLETA = BICYCLE
DE SU ABUELA PARA NAVIDAD = FROM HIS GRANDMOTHER FOR CHRISTMAS
CON SUS MANOS = WITH HIS HANDS
BICIS DE SCHWINN = SCHWINN BIKES
MI MISMO DELEITE = MY OWN DELIGHT
CONSEJO = ADVICE

¿ESTAS LISTO CON TUS MANOS? MEJOR FRENA CON TUS MANOS, NO CON TUS ZAPATOS. = ARE YOU READY WITH YOUR HANDS? BETTER TO BRAKE WITH YOUR HANDS, NOT YOUR SHOES.

SOBRINO = NEPHEW
UNA MARIPOSA = A BUTTERFLY
NADA ME TURBA = NOTHING BOTHERS ME
TÍA = AUNT
LA LLAVE = THE KEY
CON CADA UNO = WITH EACH ONE
EL RITMO = THE RHYTHM
MIS PIJAMAS = MY PAJAMAS
EN REALIDAD = IN REALITY
MI ROPA = MY CLOTHES
SOL = SUN
SOMBRA = SHADOW
LA PERRA = THE FEMALE DOG
EL BAÑO = THE BATHROOM
LOS PERROS = THE DOGS
TIENE BASTANTE SUERTE = HAVE ENOUGH LUCK
MI VOCABULARIO = MY VOCABULARY

LADRAR = TO BARK
CORREA = LEASH
PURA = PURE

LA MASCOTA DE MI UNIVERSIDAD = THE MASCOT OF MY
UNIVERSITY

TODO ES UNA MEZCLA HERMOSA DE MEMORIAS E HISTORIAS
AHORA PARA MI Y OTRA OPORTUNIDAD PARA PRACTICAR LOS
USOS DE POR Y PARA, TAREA DE MIS CLASES ESPAÑOL. = ALL
OF THIS IS A BEAUTIFUL MIX OF MEMORIES AND STORIES
NOW FOR ME AND ANOTHER OPPORTUNITY TO PRACTICE
USES OF POR AND PARA, HOMEWORK FROM MY SPANISH
CLASSES.

Day 17—Week Three of Classes

LAS BROMAS = JOKES

TIP OF THE DAY: **LAUGH. GIGGLE.**

Sonriendo y bailando, Marlene disfruta la vida.

Language is a funny, funny thing and anyone who thinks otherwise has, as my mother says, another think coming. It can only be just so clear. Yes, the relative preciseness distinguishes us from our animal friends. And brain science is narrowing in on just how language develops and happens within and between us. But the hilarity in the moment! Well you just have to be there. Take yesterday for example.

Since I had chosen el ritmo de la familia for the day, I was peacefully going about my reading and bathing, back and forth between el patio, el salón, la cocina y mi habitación and occasionally hearing amongst the swirl of language between other family members something about "nolalu." I noted that it was unusual for the television to be off (without Joaquín in front of it) but I reasoned that maybe Marlene was so sick (in her bedroom with no contact behind a closed door) that his usual routine was on hold.

This concerned me. It's not unusual for "the light to dawn on me" here slower than it does on everyone else. This was one of those times. After a long stretch on Wi-Fi with my phone, I went back to my room to recharge it and finally discovered—ah!—no electricity. "No las luces." ¡Ahora entiendo! This was a new experience for me and I was glad I had brought my flashlight and head lamp, not knowing if the disruption in service would last after the inevitable and punctual return of darkness a las seis.

Confusión en mi mente reared itself again later when cousin Janett stopped by to visit and las mujeres of three generations gathered en el salón. Even Marlene, with her very stiff back (I finally understood the nature of her dolor y enfermedad) joined us. Besides the coffee and cake offered by the younger ones to we three mayores (Marlene, Janett y yo), I suggested we also share the Christmas cookies I'd made the other night con los niños. After all I did think it was a bit strange that these cookies never surfaced as a dessert or treat when other things did.

Marlene seemed to really like this idea and it dawned on me—ah! for some reason, this is still something of mine to give away instead of, as I had assumed, family food now under her direction. Anyway, when the little tin was opened and las jovenes had quickly, with glee I might add, grabbed one, there was an immediate scream. Madelin y María José jumped up, took the tin and ran out the front door. Had the cookies molded so much that this chaos was the only appropriate response? Were they feeding the cookies to the dog? Finally a word that I understood came through amongst the cacophony, "Hormigas." There are ants everywhere here, and it's a wonder Marlene manages to keep them out of the food. Apparently, las muchachas ridded the container of the culprits sufficiently enough to everyone's satisfaction because they returned, settled themselves and proceeded to pass the tin around for everyone's pleasure. Afternoon tea en la casa de Marlene resumed with galletas de la extranjera—strange cookies indeed!

I have a friend en el campo. Se llama Bernave. El me enseñó sobre las bromas. The best ones are the ones we tell on ourselves.

Mixing Up Vowels, AGAIN!

Ok, so once when we were vacationing as a family in Costa Rica, I scooted into the front seat of the van to chat away the miles with our driver. Look out, here comes una broma on me! Instead of describing Geronimo (Clarke's assigned name in high school Spanish class) as a better ("mejor")/easier) name for Spanish speakers to pronounce than Clarke, I explained that my son, Geronimo, was a woman ("mujer"). The driver's and every other head in the van whipped around to check what I was talking about before I realized my error. And, ja ja ja, the guffawing ensued at my expense.

Later in the coffee co-operative of La Corona my host, Bernave, encouraged joke-telling for fun one evening. Most of my English riddles are a play on words that don't hold up in Spanish. However once I realized that these language stories about my own silly experiences would be understood by all, I could contribute funnies too and the laughter continued.

GLOSSARY

CAPTION = SMILING AND DANCING, MARLENE ENJOYS LIFE.

MI HABITACIÓN = MY ROOM

LAS LUCES = THE LIGHTS

¡AHORA ENTIENDO! = NOW I UNDERSTAND!

CONFUSIÓN EN MI MENTE = CONFUSION IN MY MIND

LAS MUJERES = THE WOMEN

DOLOR Y ENFERMEDAD = PAIN AND SICKNESS

MAYORES = ELDERS

LOS NIÑOS = THE CHILDREN

LAS JOVENES = THE TEENAGERS

HORMIGAS = ANTS

GALLETAS DE LA EXTRANJERA = THE FOREIGNER'S COOKIES

EN EL CAMPO = IN THE COUNTRY

SE LLAMA = HE'S CALLED

ÉL ME ENSEÑÓ SOBRE LAS BROMAS = HE TAUGHT ME ABOUT JOKES

JA JA JA = HA HA HA

Day 18—December 30

El fregadero y agua filtrada en la cocina de Marlene

There appears to be plenty of agua pressure this morning, as both faucets en mi ducha y lavabo are dripping and overfilling the buckets beneath them. And while the toilet flushes easily, the overhead light in mi cuarto no funciona. It appears the bulb has burned out because the outlet de electricidad I'm using to recharge my phone is putting out juice. All is well nonetheless. I have my headlamp and the light is expanding outside my no-longer-shaded ventanas. Plus I don't have as much time to write because I composed three longer email messages in the wee hours. Those messages are now waiting in an e-queue somewhere to send later in the morning when I have Wi-Fi again. The first connection is available al lado de casa de Marlene at su hermana Lylian's house, which I walk by as I leave Marlene's.

Last night while I was talking with Carolina, mi teléfono died, which means my balance of international minutes expired. Bless Marlene, she loaned me a phone and every few days I recharge it with minutes. Then las muchachas help me figure out (very roughly) mi saldo. Once Diana helped me by simply taking my phone in hand, pressing a few buttons and—poof!—successful use of the bono from Moviestar, one of the two cellular phone companies in Nicaragua.

Thanks to Diana, I had 60 more international minutes "gratis." Today one of the grand joys that awaits me is visiting Claró, the other phone company. Freddy, my agent at Matagalpa Tours, guesses there will be better phone service on the coast through Claró. I will inevitably live through yet another "fun" experiencia en comunicación when I negotiate obtaining a microchip (same word in Spanish, just different pronunciation of the i's, as long e's) for my iPhone. Alas, after varying degrees of consternation I have to return Marlene's phone that, I'll admit, I now have a certain fondness for.*

I'm happy to say that I think my dinero situation is sufficient, por lo menos for the duration of my time in Matagalpa. I settled my tuition bill yesterday in very crisp 20's from the ATM, an important requirement. Travelers are advised to bring perfect bills as those with any tears whatsoever are often not accepted and at the very least, scrutinized. A coyote did accept two old twenty-dollar bills from me after Colibrí had to reject them but I wouldn't count on a coyote again. I also withdrew dollars and córdobas for the festivities and travels ahead. While I have been using my VISA infrequently here, it was accepted in the crafts store that Escuela Colíbri y Matagalpa Tours share. I purchased woven pencil cases for my writer friends at this colorful shop.

By the way, you might ask, "Who are the coyotes?" Come to Nicaragua and find out.

*Later Marlene decided to lend me the phone for the coast with the understanding that Lynn and Richard would return it.

Telares Nicaragua

Author's Note: I found this sales tag on the pencil cases I purchased at the Colibrí/Matagalpa Tours shop. Spanish was on one side and the English translation was on the other.

Estos tejidos son elaborados por un grupo de tejedoras de la comunidad Indígena El Chile, ubicada en las montañas a 30 kms de Matagalpa. A partir de los años 80's hemos rescatado nuestra tradición de tejer en telares. Con las telas confeccionamos carteras, mochilas, bolsos, monederos, billeteras . . . Somos mujeres campesinas y la venta de nuestra artesanía significa para nuestras familias un ingreso muy importante que nos permite mejorar nuestras condiciones de vida.
www.telaresnicaragua.com

Nicaraguan Weavings

These textiles are made by a group of weavers in the indigenous community of El Chile, located in the mountains 30 kms from Matagalpa. In the 1980's, we rediscovered our weaving traditions. Today we produce purses, backpacks, bags, coinpurses, wallets . . . We are campesina women and the sale of our handicrafts is a very important source of income for our families, allowing us to improve our standard of living.
www.telaresnicaragua.com

GLOSSARY

CAPTION = THE KITCHEN SINK AND FILTERED WATER IN MARLENE'S KITCHEN

EN MI DUCHA Y LAVABO = IN MY SHOWER AND SINK

MI CUARTO = MY ROOM

NO FUNCIONA = IT DOESN'T WORK

VENTANAS = WINDOWS

AL LADO DE = BESIDE

MI SALDO = MY BALANCE

HERMANA = SISTER

BONO = BONUS

GRATIS = FREE

EXPERIENCIA EN COMUNICACIÓN = EXPERIENCE IN COMMUNICATION

Day 19—New Year's Eve

VERBS = LOS VERBOS

TIP OF THE DAY: **TRUST IN YOUR TEACHERS.**

Mi maestra Diana en la Escuela Colibrí

Truthfully, New Year's Eve is my least favorite holiday. Once, Rob's cousin and best man in our wedding, Scott, and his bride Michelle, got married on New Year's Eve. That party was a blast. But the rest of the usual hoopla—drinking, partying, staying up until midnight no matter what—was never my thing, at least not recently. In the EEUU, especially with teens/young adults in the house, I was just glad to talk with folks the next day and realize everyone had gotten home safely. What terrible premonitions to bring to this night of festivities! So far, in the early evening, the day could not have been more different.

After a two day introduction to some of the subjunctive tenses in Spanish, including Presente Perfecto, Pretérito Imperfecto, Pretérito

Pluscuamperfecto, Diana realized I'd be much better served if we backtracked to a review of Condicional Tenses (Simple, Condicional Progresive y Condicional Perfecto) to end our time together. She called them "Flash" lessons, at which she is exceptionally good. Unlike the Subjunctive tenses that were piling up in my mind in an absolute crowded mess so that I could no longer correctly put "Yo tengo" or "Quiero ir al baño" together, I was able to follow her clear, logical description of the Condicional Tenses and can now listen for them as I read and converse. Maybe with some study I can even incorporate them sometimes into my own humble comments.

Or maybe not. There are ways around los verbos that I've been using for a long time. My Spanish after all, according to my daughter, is "huevos afuera" (this expression is not in the glossary.) It's what an extrovert does who desperately wants to converse but hasn't studied Spanish from the ground up in structured classes.

I also appreciated Diana's beautiful response to my request to translate six sentences I use often on a form letter at my work site. I have always felt awkward about using English on a Spanish form. There was also time to review pronombres. Thus I am leaving my classes today with some hope of correctly incorporating me, te, la, lo, les, los, nos y se. We'll see.

But the best part was, given the one-on-one structure of Escuela Colibrí, we also interspersed conversations throughout the grammar lessons—about faith, education, cultural differences, my upcoming trip to the coast, my telephone and anything else that came to mind. It really made for a lovely morning and a satisfying end to my studies. Of course I wish I could take mi amiga along with me on mi hombro to whisper en mi oreja and coach me as needed while I continue to learn Spanish (including not saying hombre or hambre when what I mean is shoulder).

But instead I will take Diana along in my heart forever and always. She's there with Susan and Maria, mis maestras de Español. I will be agradecida to them para siempre.

La Escuela de Español Colibrí

(de www.colibrispanishschool.com)

¿Estás buscando una ciudad tranquila con cosas lindas para hacer y a la vez estudiar español en un ambiente muy agradable y con calidad profesional? Entonces, te espera un lugar con instructoras nicaragüenses con experiencia en la enseñanza del español, con capacidad de español conversar en español sobre diversos temas, con mente abierta, criterio propio, felices de compartir sus conocimientos, enseñar su idioma y aprender de otras culturas y experiencias.

Nuestra Escuela de Español Colibrí te ofrece clases de español para grupos y/o particulares y también en paquetes. Con los paquetes incluimos: clases uno a uno o en grupo, libros de estudio, alojamiento en casa de una familia matagalpina, actividades que incluyen caminatas a reservas naturales, visitas a museos, organizaciones sociales, centros de estudios, fábrica de chocolate y actividades personalizadas según tus intereses. GRATIS para estudiantes de español.

Colibrí Spanish School
(English translation from www.colibrispanishschool.com)

Are you looking for a fun, pleasant, professional, and dynamic place to study Spanish? Come to the Colibrí Spanish School. Imagine a place with credentialed, native Spanish language teachers who are open-minded and able to engage in critical discussions; trained professionals who are excited to engage in cultural exchanges.

Colibrí Spanish School in Matagalpa, Nicaragua offers group and/or private Spanish classes, as well as customized package programs. Packages include: Spanish classes, textbooks, lodging with a Matagalpan family, activities such as hikes through natural reserves, museum visits, tours of local organizations and businesses, as well as personalized activities based on your interests. FREE (for Spanish students): Traditional Nicaraguan dishes every Tuesday, yoga classes every Wednesday, games and dancing every Friday, planned group activities and excursions, studying materials, coffee, tea, Wi-Fi, laptops, tourist information, walks during class hours to visit museums, local markets, lookouts over the city, etc.

GLOSSARY

CAPTION = My teacher, Diana, at Colibrí School

Presente Perfecto, Pretérito Imperfecto, Pretérito Pluscuamperfecto = Present Perfect, Imperfect, Past Perfect

Condicional = Conditional

Condicional Progresivo y Condicional Perfecto = Conditional Progressive and Conditional Perfect

Yo tengo = I have
Quiero ir al baño = I want to go to the bathroom.
Pronombres = Pronouns

Me, te, la, lo, les, los, nos y se = Me, you, it, him, them, us and himself (and many other things)

Mi hombro = My shoulder
En mi oreja = In my ear
Hombre = Man
Hambre = Hunger
Mis maestras de Español = My Spanish teachers
Agradecida = Grateful
Para siempre = Forever

Day 20—Adios 2014

THE OLD ONE = EL VIEJO

TIP OF THE DAY: **DELIGHT.**

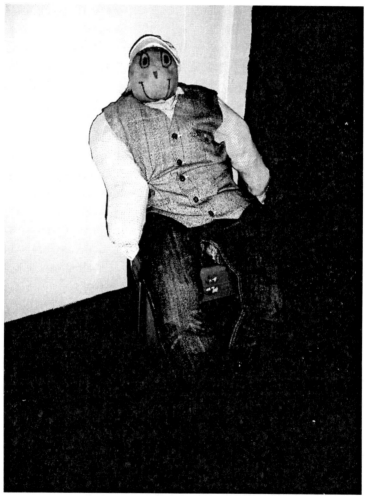

El viejo nos recibió en la fiesta de Año Nuevo.

After two or three hours of dancing and drinking and eating with the women and children of la familia at Janett's home, I was wearing thin. My Spanish in a fiesta environment is insufficient to say the least. And then a las once, Marlene packed up her younger ones to head home giving me the clear direction to stay. As Rob and my kids will tell you, I am decidedly not a late bird. Most days, I am up before everyone else and fold my tent early at the close of day. When my kids heard I'd had a Toña at 2:30 a.m. Christmas morning, I could hear their jaws drop two continents away. Still by now, Xiomara and María José, Marlene's hermana y su hija, had arrived after the long New Year's misa. I was more familiar with these two so the dancing and the nibbling continued.

On the way into Janett's home, I had been introduced to El Viejo, a life-sized scarecrow-like muñeco, and I understood enough to know he represented the soon-to-be El Año Viejo—2014. Maybe they told me more about the midnight procedures, maybe not.

But a medianoche, the perfunctory rocket bombs and firecrackers started going off all over town—no surprise there. And everyone started, somewhat frantically, looking for 20-something-year-old, long and lean Herson. I surmised he and El Viejo had a date coming up—perhaps a parade in the streets or something. When Herson did show up, he immediately grabbed the doll, threw him over his shoulder, delivered him to the middle of the street, doused him with gasoline and lit him on fire—all to the shrieks of la familia's party-goers and several other vecinos. Eduardo, a burly and spirited 12-year-old, surfaced again with handfuls of bottle rockets. He proceeded to add one or two at a time to the diminishing muñeco and the growing bonfire. All this in a stiff wind. My feeble questions led me to believe this scene was happening in barrios all over town.

I have to admit that this dangerous enactment was thrilling to me. Talk about wide awake! Even as I wondered if our heros, Herson y Eduardo—quite the pair—would get out of this alive, at least only losing un dedo or two, I shrieked and guffawed with the rest of them. Yet another wonderful surprise, brought to me through immersion with this fabulous cast of characters including El Viejo.

¡Adios, Señor 2014. Bienvenido el bebé!

Pardon Me!

I will never be able to order Nicaragua's beer, Toña, again without smiling since I have incorrectly asked for a coña (female body part) instead of a caña, cup-size beer, in Spain. Fortunately I was with Clarke at the time. I haven't always been careful enough about pronouncing vowels correctly when speaking Spanish. This is a critical skill for making oneself understood. Lucky for me, when I proceeded to order "tres coñas"—rhymes with Toñas, get it?—Clarke was along to correct me and quell any snickers. Ever the teacher, he later suggested that if I had used a few more words, for example, "Quiero tres coñas," I would have likely been understood by the bartender regardless of how vulgar my pronunciation was.

And in deference to male-female balance: For the same reason when traveling in Latin America sola, I use my full name, Penélope. That's because the shortened version, Penny, can easily be mispronounced as pene (male body part). Been there, done that.

GLOSSARY

CAPTION = THE OLD MAN WELCOMED US AT THE NEW YEAR'S EVE PARTY.

FIESTA = PARTY
A LAS ONCE = AT 11 O'CLOCK
SU HIJA = HER DAUGHTER
CONVERSACIONES = CONVERSATIONS
MUÑECO = DOLL
AÑO = YEAR
A MEDIANOCHE = AT MIDNIGHT
UN DEDO = A FINGER
¡ADIOS, SEÑOR 2014. BIENVENIDO EL BEBÉ! = GOODBYE, MR. 2014. WELCOME THE BABY!
SOLA = ALONE

Day 21—Welcome 2015

SWIMMING POOL = LA PISCINA

TIP OF THE DAY: **BE ADOPTED.**

Viajé con los jóvenes en la parte de atrás de la camioneta.

I am writing early this morning on the transition day—our travel day to Corn Island. While I had been expecting a day off on January 1st—no classes, no schedule, no expectations, another quiet day at home with la familia—that didn't happen. Yes, I was very much looking forward to some downtime but I wouldn't trade the last two days of special activities for anything. And without that day off, I am two days behind in my writing. Sounds like I am already stateside again y demasiado ocupada. One blessing is that even with all the goings-on, me siento mejor in terms of the cold and cough. And I managed to take care of the business details that needed to happen before my upcoming trip including getting cash for Marlene's tip and cash in dollars and córdobas for traveling. I also confirmed international and local minutes on the phone, as best as I can tell at least.

I had a good talk with Mom and Dad too. Dad is now using a wheelchair full time, though still fighting it, and they have moved a hospital bed into their condo at the retirement community. They are certainly experiencing a much bigger transition than I am. I am amazed that he is still managing to live "at home," a goal my folks have both wanted all along. Maybe he will even die at home and I will be present for that. ¿Quién sabe?

Wow, it is really raining outside! Reminds me of last night. After hanging our ropa de nadar out to dry, we were all sitting around en el salón, telling those who'd stayed at home about our day at El Ranchón. Suddenly a fantastic viento y lluvia sprang up out of nowhere and, as at other times, las jóvenes jumped up amongst much language chaos. This time I caught on after only a second or two, swept up in the excitement of entendiendo and rushed to move our clothes. I have noticed that there isn't much rushing here or, at least, it's not constant like it is at home.

Sure, everyone can hop to, as witnessed last night but usually there is a gradual magnetic pull one direction or another that gets folks places roughly, or not, on time. Yesterday, Marlene had emphasized that her cousin was punctual. Furthermore, Janett was borrowing a truck from her office that Joaquín would drive to la piscina that was located in, I thought, nearby San Ramón. We were to be ready to leave exactly at 10 a.m. Interestingly, the one part of the scenario that I imagined correctly and surprisingly, given how casual folks usually are about punctuality, was the timely getaway.

I get the feeling that Janett is una jefa of sorts; she certainly manages all los jóvenes in her charge with reasonable efficiency. What I misconstrued in my expectations was the rest of the story. Our trip was to La Dahlia, 45 kilómetros away (and more than an hour) over a good but winding highway through gorgeous mountain countryside. Our conveyance was una camioneta but not my alternating flashes between minivan comfort and crowding a dozen of us into a truck's cab. Instead we rode in relative comfort, like soldiers of old did. Joaquín, Marlene and Janett rode in the cab and I sat on benches with the oldest tía/abuela Mercedes, 78, and the six teenage cousins.

Fortunately the truck sported a frame and heavy canvas covering; therefore through the mix of rain and sun we rode in relative comfort. There were no seat belts so there was a lot of slipping and sliding. As we drove out of town, unknown muchachos de las calles jumped on our back bumper a couple of times to ride up hills. And I uttered a distinct oración and acknowledgement: "Vamos adelante. Nosotros estamos en las manos de Dios y específicamente, en este minuto, en las manos de Joaquín. ¡Que Dios, nos proteja!

Our destination was fantastic! "Una piscina" was an insufficient description. I realized when we arrived that Marlene had shown me photos of another huésped con la familia at this location. She had probably then told me that we could all go back to this fabulous water park/playground, but until this moment I had not completely understand the prologue for our plan on New Year's Day.

Apparently El Ranchón is a man-made lagoon, developed and owned by Nicaraguans. I have to say that while I certainly felt welcome there, I was the only extranjera in the crowd, at least the only very fair-skinned one. The others appeared to be Latinos with resources and of the upper or growing (hopefully) middle class. Another thing that I had understood was Marlene's request that, instead of taking the family out for helado, I cover their entry fees for using the facilities. That was an interesting arrangement in itself: $5(US) to don the pink plastic pulsera and swim in the pool and $10(US) para llevar la pulsera verde to use the giant blow-up play structures y barcos en la laguna. There was no charge to sit alongside and pay only for drinks and food, if desired, including full meals from the casual poolside restaurant y parrilla.

Yes, the ex-salvavidas in me shivered occasionally because there were glass bottles poolside and an insufficient number of lifejackets. Plus our kids who couldn't swim a lick (apparently) were wearing these lifejackets to paddle around the la piscina. Still, for the most part, I loved it and was agradecida that I had not let my post Flor de Caña nausea keep me at home. Because of my cold, I shied away from buying a bracelet at first, as I would have been happy to sit in one of the few lounge chairs (like the princess I am), reading mi revista in the dappled sol/sombra all afternoon.

I came to my senses soon enough though when I saw the paddleboats and individual kayaks (incluído con the green bracelet), reasoning that I could tool around the lagoon, communing with nature, enjoying myself, and still stay dry. Best laid plans. While my first trip with Janett in the paddleboat was dry and uneventful, I managed to capsize myself while getting into the kayak. That caused another one of those immediate all-family-members-on-deck routines. Thank God they all came to my rescue and were there to retrieve mis sandalias, gorro, y lentes. I am less thrilled to say that they all watched me somehow get back on the dock without a ladder and without hurting myself. Kudos to Jackson, the slight but infinitely strong boat steward. He was even willing to launch me a second time. As I gingerly, carefully seated myself for the second round, I realized how mindless I had been the first time thinking, "Oh, kayaking. I do this. No hay problema." Disaster averted and I enjoyed two quiet laps around the laguna among los gansos and parakeets. ¡Qué exquisito!

AND on the ride home, during an especially magnificent atardecer, we enjoyed a complete double arcoiris, very appropriate for my last evening with this fabulous familia nicarangüese. Entonces, bienvenido 2015 y adios Matagalpa.

Transformational Travel Mission Purpose Statement—Saint Mark's Cathedral Church in the World in 2011

Author's Note: This was submitted to the Church in the World Coordinating Committee at Saint Mark's Cathedral.

Transformational Travel is a new and growing ministry centered on creating community through travel. As we plan trips and travel in small groups, our goal is to be educated and transformed by people whose lives are different than our own. Our intention is to build mutual relationships in all the countries we visit and learn about the material conditions under which "most people" live.

GLOSSARY

CAPTION = I TRAVELED WITH THE TEENAGERS IN THE BACK OF THE TRUCK.

DEMASIADO OCUPADA = TOO BUSY
ME SIENTO MEJOR = I FEEL BETTER
¿QUIÉN SABE? = WHO KNOWS?
ROPA DE NADAR = SWIMSUITS
VIENTO = WIND
LLUVIA = RAIN
ENTENDIMIENTO = UNDERSTANDING
UNA JEFA = FEMALE BOSS
UNA CAMIONETA = SMALL TRUCK
MUCHACHOS = YOUNG FELLOWS
CALLES = THE STREETS
ORACIÓN = PRAYER

VAMOS ADELANTE. NOSOTROS ESTAMOS EN LAS MANOS DE DIOS Y ESPECIFICAMENTE, EN ESTE MINUTO, EN LAS MANOS DE JOAQUÍN. ¡QUÉ DIOS, NOS PROTEJA! = LET'S GO FORWARD. WE ARE IN GOD'S HANDS AND SPECIFICALLY IN THIS MINUTE, IN JOAQUÍN'S HANDS. GOD PROTECT US!

HUÉSPED = GUEST
PULSERA = BRACELET
LLEVAR = WEAR
VERDE = GREEN
BARCOS = BOATS
LAGUNA = LAGOON
PARRILLA = GRILL
SALVAVIDAS = LIFEGUARD
FLOR DE CAŇA = NICARAGUAN RUM
MI REVISTA = MY MAGAZINE
INCLUÍDO = INCLUDED WITH
MIS SANDALIAS = MY SANDALS
GORRO = CAP
LENTES = GLASSES
NO HAY PROBLEMA = NO PROBLEM
LOS GANSOS = THE GEESE
¡QUÉ EXQUISITO! = HOW EXQUISITE!
ATARDECER = LATE AFTERNOON
ARCOIRIS = RAINBOW
ENTONCES = THEN

Day 22—Transitioning by the Sea

ISLAND = LA ISLA

TIP OF THE DAY: **UNPLUG.**

Comimos y jugamos en los restaurantes de Big Corn Island.
(de izquierda a derecha) Yo, Lynn y Richard

So here I am finally writing again three days later beside the Caribbean Sea on Big Corn Island. I have stuck my toes into the waves and am now propped in a lounge chair under a palm tree in a warm, sweet brisa. Finally I am settling here after packing and unpacking twice in 24 hours. I was right, bringing as few things as possible was a good strategy but I still have a suitcase (mostly clothes and gifts at this point) and a backpack (mostly books and my electronic paraphernalia including the laptop from work as I am hoping to type a draft of this booklet before returning home) and my purse (with most of the valuable items I'd want if the plane goes down in enemy territory or something).

Fortunately, I bought an ever-expanding purse when I was at Matagalpa Tours the last time around, another item created by the indigenous weavers. What I especially like about it, besides its strength and ever-expanding characteristic, is that it includes a large zipper with an overall cover plus two more zippers, one of which closes off an interior pouch just the right size for my passport and my phones. Not only are they safe this way, I don't have to fish around in the bottom of the bag every time I want to use them, which is often. The third zipper closes the money pouch which is attached to the interior purse just inside the larger opening by a long cord so that I can easily retrieve money as needed. Plus it stays attached to the purse, "no matter what." I no longer feel the need to wear a money belt— ah, progress.

As I write, I realize that about 24 hours ago I was still in Matagalpa saying goodbye to the fabulous team—una buena pareja—of Marlene and Joaquín. My friends Lynn and Richard were picking me up in their truck (driven by Francisco, their primary employee who learned to drive and secured his permit under their tutelage) to go to the riotous bus station and catch the express bus to Managua. Talk about brilliant luck. My extranjero tour guides had bought $C72—about $3(US)—tickets to secure our assigned-seat reservation. And Freddy from Matagalpa Tours was also on the bus (unexpectedly) as he was heading to the airport to meet another group of travelers. Again, I could not have planned it better. Best to just jump in the river and relax.

The afternoon La Costeña flight from Managua to la isla was flawless and I began to recognize how exhausted I was during the deep 20-minute siesta that the loud prop plane afforded me. It was as if I was being rocked in familiar arms. No surprise that I slept 10 hours straight upon landing in our one-night-transition hotel until space became available in the ideal Al Paraíso Beach Hotel, complete with grass-roofed cabinas and lounge chairs by the sea.

As I expected, Lynn and Richard are proving to be wonderful travel companions. For one thing, they speak Spanish better than I do. They are also really interested in exploring La Costa del Caribe with me. Maybe I can even keep up with their brilliant conversations. They retired from the fields of medicine and environmental engineering and they continue to be complete students of the world, reading and considering global issues, online, plugged in.

I, on the other hand, am still finding the Moviestar phone to be a challenge. While it says I have a balance of $28(US) available for international calls, I am not able to connect with Lynn or Richard or with anyone back home. I have just about decided to really unplug and simply rely on Facebook/email via Wi-Fi for this Corn Island stretch. Maybe we will even pull off a Skype connection or two.

What a Paranoid Optimist Can Fit in the Right Purse

- water bottle,
- passport,
- cash,
- bug repellent,
- camera,
- phone,
- Kleenex,
- cough drops to foil public health should there be any concern about my lingering-and-still-TB-sounding cough,
- mi diccionario,
- mi diario,
- an ink pen and some post-its,
- my thumb brace to ward off arthritis pain when I write,
- a couple of panty liners just in case,
- a laminated copy of the Lord's Prayer in Spanish,
- audiophones and, ta da,
- ear plugs.

GLOSSARY

CAPTION = WE ATE AND PLAYED IN BIG CORN ISLAND'S
RESTAURANTS. (LEFT TO RIGHT—ME, LYNN AND RICHARD)

BRISA = BREEZE

UNA BUENA PAREJA = A FINE PAIR

CABINAS = CABINS

LA COSTA DEL CARIBE = THE CARIBBEAN COAST

Day 23—Around Corn Island

BICYCLE = LA BICICLETA

TIP OF THE DAY: EXERCISE.

Alquilé la bicicleta de la maestra y recorrí toda la isla.

Ah, another Sunday. This time church was island-style. I have started my 2015 morning practice with reflective journaling and contemplation. This year I'm starting with a text in English and a journal with notes in Spanish (Diario con Jesús by Sarah Hornsby). Settling into el ritmo of each book here on Corn Island, where I am essentially sola, suits me.

Since yesterday, I have almost followed mi propio consejo and given up on Skype and on Moviestar for international calls. The Wi-Fi at the hotel's restaurant and that which I stumble across occasionally, like at a small island restaurant called Marlene's Roadside Café (I'm not kidding!) where I stopped for lunch today, seems sufficient to keep a slight hold on life at home in the states. There are reports of 10-plus inches of snow. Others write that they are taking down their Christmas decorations before the kids return to school which—OMG!—I just realized happens tomorrow!

Here in surreal island-time-and-space, after rising early, reading, writing and meditating some, I joined one of the Dutch owners of Paraíso and her friend from Hungary for yoga, seaside under palm trees. What a gift. And then, after breakfast, I connected with the teacher who shares my duplex cabina, and settled on a $5(US) rental fee to borrow her near-new, one-speed, brakes-on-the-pedals, upright bicicleta. I set out on my own to discover this 10 km-long island, mostly following the beach route. I stopped frequently to check the guidebook and read stories about the milestones I passed. The island is flat for the most part but a few times I had the chance to stand up and pedal like a kid in order to mount the inclines instead of walking up.

Even though I'm still in Nicaragua, the scenery and lifestyle has changed completely...mountains versus coast, the life of a tourist instead of a homestay guest with a local family, and much more English spoken around me. I have learned that many people in these communities support their families by working on cruise ships for many months of the year due to their bilingual prowess. It seems as if my little adopted country will keep surprising and delighting me. However now I miss two families—mine in Seattle and Marlene's in Matagalpa.

Back to the bike—besides the magnificent, show-stopping views, it occurred to me early on that another highlight of this particular paseo would be checking out the various restaurants that had been recommended. I'm happy to say that after a disappointing cena at Fisher's Cave on our first night on the island, we met our stride with last night's pescado a la plancha at Al Paraíso's Buccaneer. Tonight we are following the recommendation of at least three to enjoy Italian food at La Princesa.

After my island tour I'm recommending drinks at Casa Canada y la comida y cervezas (maybe dancing too?) next door at the casual sand-floor, Jimmy-Buffett-style Spekito's. Richard and Lynn are food connoisseurs so it's a bit nervy of me to call the shots in the eating and drinking departments, but really, I don't think we can go wrong. The highlight of mi paseo, hands-down, was literally stumbling on the very packed Saint James Episcopal Church at the end of Sunday misa. Niños were serving as acolytes with cross and incense. I arrived in time to join the singing of The First Noel in English and watch the recession. Afterwards, I was warmly welcomed by Vicar Adrian Benedict. While I was decidedly underdressed, he emphasized, "We are Episcopalians. Welcome! No worries!"

Now I am watching gray clouds roll in for the second time today. I had been drenched once already while bike riding. And the surf is rough; apparently there were no boats to Little Corn Island today and probably not tomorrow either. That sounds like a great excuse to do absolutely nothing. Estoy tranquila—why mess with that?

To You of the Red Carpet

Author's Note: I wrote this poem long ago when I was away from Saint Mark's, my church home on Sunday morning. Even so I was able to enjoy a similar service because the liturgy of the Anglican/Episcopal Communion has the same basic structure everywhere in the world including Corn Island. At Saint Mark's children and families can sit quietly on a carpet beside the pews and read, draw, listen and sing with their parents as la misa unfolds.

To You of the Red Carpet,

In this Holy Week, I am away from you

　　　　thinking of the antics of the children amongst you

　　　　who show me

God's Profound Love every Sunday.

Mostly I want you to know that if you persist,

wade through the short nights and the early mornings,

and somehow dress them and yourselves and come anyway

at 9 a.m.

to pray and sing and listen. . . .

If you do this for years and years,

you will find friends beside you whom you will celebrate with—

Life,

their marriages,

and yes, deaths and resurrections too.

And if you negotiate with these same children as teenagers

to keep a string or two attached,

You may hear her reading God's Word to you

in another language

Or him playing dance tunes for you at church on Mardi Gras.

And even when you are in a strange town

away from home like I am,

perhaps where these same red-carpet children have taken you –

anywhere in the world –

You can find the skeleton of this liturgy and Holy, Holy Story

nearby.

There will always be people of the red carpet

who have watched and applauded as the children have grown,

And these children will be there too

the ones who are worshiping beside you

in their own blessed ways.

As they gurgle and wiggle and absorb

and are absorbed in

This Heart of Love –

square and red for now

plush and soft –

Yours and mine and God's

Forever.

GLOSSARY

CAPTION = I RENTED THE TEACHER'S BICYCLE AND TRAVELED AROUND THE ISLAND.

EL RITMO = RHYTHM
MI PROPIO CONSEJO = MY OWN ADVICE
PASEO = RIDE
CENA = DINNER
PESCADO A LA PLANCHA = GRILLED FISH
CERVEZAS = BEERS
ESTOY TRANQUILA. = I'M CALM.

Day 24—Rough Seas in Paradise and in my Heart, Last Day at Al Paraíso

I STRUGGLE. = FORCEJO.

TIP OF THE DAY: **WRITE A POEM.**

Con mar agitado no hay viajes a los cayos o a Little Corn Island.

As happy as I have been here on Corn Island, I have been equally sorrowful.

As full of ease as yesterday was, today is difficult.

My Skype call with Rob—ah, finally success!—was interrupted repeatedly.

And, of course, el vendedor said my English is better than my Spanish.

Why would that cut like a knife? My English is better.

I was inconvenienced repeatedly, even after a profound sleep.

I did not expect esta lucha, again and again.

Simply, spelled out, life is about realizing Goodness.

Still, con la facilidad of being, forcejo repeatedly.

I am rereading my poem, the very most I could write when I sat down in this lounge chair by the sea after as much of an altercation as I've had in these three-plus weeks. I was asked to move rooms for this last remaining night at Al Paraíso. Perhaps because I am the one mujer sola, I was asked to pack and move to another resort room, before moving to a whole new location and packing and unpacking tomorrow, all in less than 24 hours. This wasn't what Matagalpa Tours had arranged, I'm sure of it. I just couldn't see it and so I said no.

As I write, I realize how very much I miss Rob and how much I crave a long private conversation with him, por lo menos.

And one frustration brings up another. Estoy tan triste that my Spanish is so pitiful. What was I expecting? Un milagro, for heaven's sake?! When we are infants and toddlers, language comes to us as a shared medium that surrounds us. To learn a new version of this characteristic that separates us from the other species (along with our opposable thumbs) takes valor, commitment, disciplina y mucho tiempo. Today, I do not know if I can stomach much more.

So what's a discouraged vieja to do, heavy-hearted beside the sea? The newlyweds, returning from a swim, recommended a dip and agreed to watch my bag and clothes as I discarded them on the sand. Sports bra and panties framed my pale belly for the plunge and I took the welcome hand of a jolly, also rolly-like-me, brown-skinned chico as he led me beyond the surf and into the refreshing, suave salt water. We bobbed along with sus amigos y menores. Like una muchacha joven, I washed my cares away under a colorful puesta del sol and rising full moon. Adiós último día on Corn Island.

Matagalpa Tours

Author's Note: Each time I have traveled in Nicaragua I have gladly used the services of Matagalpa Tours. This fine locally-owned and operated company describes themselves like this:

"Matagalpa Tours is a Nicaraguan tour operator specialized in creating sustainable travel experiences, connecting nature, adventure and social-cultural activities. We can provide your customized tour around Nicaragua and we are the experts for authentic destinations in the Central region, Northern mountains and Caribbean."

Visit www.matagalpatours.com to view gorgeous photos and for additional detailed information in Spanish or in English.

GLOSSARY

CAPTION = A CHOPPY SEA SO THERE ARE NO TRIPS TODAY TO THE KEYS OR LITTLE CORN ISLAND

EL VENDEDOR = THE SALESMAN
ESTA LUCHA = THIS FIGHT
LA FACILIDAD = EASE
ESTOY TAN TRISTE = I AM SO SAD
DISCIPLINA = DISCIPLINE
TIEMPO = TIME
VIEJA = OLD WOMAN
CHICO = BOY CHILD
SUAVE = SOFT
MENORES = YOUNGER ONES
ÚLTIMO = LAST

Day 25—Pearl Lagoon

THE EDGE OF NOWHERE = EL BORDE DE NINGUNA PARTE

TIP OF THE DAY: **KNOW WHERE YOUR FLASHLIGHT IS.**

Nos quedamos en Queen Lobster en Pearl Lagoon.

Wow! Unbelievable! I find myself wishing I was an exquisite writer who could adequately describe el borde de ninguna parte we've found. Just when I thought Nicaragua could not take me by surprise again. ¡Qué tonta!

We left Corn Island this morning heading for Bluefields en un avión pequeño. Along with our carry-on equipaje and in front of God and everyone, the 14 of us were weighed (to assure the plane would take off, I suppose). I gritted my teeth in anticipation of a rough ride in the stiff wind back to the istmo of mainland Nicaragua and was pleasantly surprised at the sweet, scenic 45-minute flight.

Then after hunting down a cash machine that would give us money (the first one didn't), we headed to the dock for our boat trip up the river to Pearl Lagoon. And what a ride it was! Our panga-style marine conveyance was a simple and practical fiberglass skiff, approximately 30 feet long and 8 feet wide. The bow in this type of boat sports a rounded point to cut through the water and a deeper hull space to accommodate luggage and such. Behind is a squared stern to support a giant outboard motor.

Our open vessel seated twenty on five benches, so four across. With regular-sized adults, it was tight; my shoulders were smooshed against my neighbors. I should have suspected some excitement when the locals on either side of me strapped on the orange horseshoe salvavidas they were given. I followed suit—after all, when in Rome. ... Moments later I estuve agradecida for my seatmates—likely crammed together like this, I would not pop out.

Two seconds after leaving el muelle and pointing north to the open sea, we planed at 35 knots and hit the wind face on with a vengeance. Next it was pouring and the clear plastic sheet stuffed on one side of us made the first of five or six trips back-and-forth over our heads. Propped above our heads and secured only with our hands, the plastic rattled loudly to beat the band. We shared several close-quarter squalls under that tarp, coming up for fresh sweet air whenever the rain stopped. At one point it did occur to me, "I hope I like Pearl Lagoon because I might just stay there until the sky clears and la brisa is tranquila. That's when I'll make my break."

Then we arrived at the Queen Lobster. The restaurant itself is situated on stilts, down a long dock and over the sea. Further out, a tiny muelle extends and harbors two little bungalows. The whole arrangement is not unlike what I'd expect to see in Thailand.

Now I have located my headlamp and extra flashlight. I have lowered my mosquito net to be ready for dark and sleeping, quizás soon after nightfall. Espero que las olas me canten durante toda la noche.

Jubilee, Liberation from Debt and Poverty

By Betsy Bell

Author's Note: At this point in my trip, more and more often I thought about home and how I could possibly begin to translate this transformative experience into my life back in the states. I was glad to have examples like my 75-year-old friend Betsy Bell who traveled in February, 2012 with me and the granddaughter she writes about below. In this essay, Betsy describes the poverty she witnessed throughout the country when she visited for the first time, twelve years before the trip we took together.

My heart ached and tears came as I watched a nurse examine a child's swollen jaw. He squirmed on his mother's lap in the concrete block room dimly lit from one open window. A metal desk with a tray of scissors, tweezers, a roll of bandages—the collection of things we Americans would find in our own bathroom cupboards—were the only tools the nurse had. She looked exhausted.

The nurse later told us she had worked half a day for pay in a clinic across the barrio and now volunteered her services in this poor part of Managua.

Later in a church, our group clustered in a doorway gazing into the large open sanctuary. On the wall a vibrant poster declared *Jubileo!* It depicted a nurse serving a family in a clinic, fully equipped and flooded with light.

What does this mean, *Jubileo?* Jubilee, explained a priest, is the year of the Lord's favor, liberation from debt, from bondage, from poverty imposed by financial institutions' austerity measures in order to extract debt payments.

This experience in 1999 while traveling with my 18-month-old granddaughter and the Saint Mark's Girls' Choir set me on a path, first to learn about the economic hardships imposed by the World Bank and the International Monetary Fund (IMF) and then to join Global South's Jubilee Movement. Nica people we met knew about the deals their government made with the IMF. They knew why their nurses were not paid enough to live on. They were part of an international network of people demanding forgiveness of odious debts. I had to help.

Weeks later, at the Seattle gathering of the World Trade Organization, ten thousand supporters of debt cancellation for poor countries formed a human chain around the Seattle King Dome's plenary meeting of the international trade delegations. I served as a marshal for the march, working side by side with labor union members, church people, progressives wanting an open transparent system for international finance.

Leaders from Nicaragua, the Philippines, South Africa, Kenya and Zambia continue to lead us northern nations to push for reforms that invite full participation of the people most affected by their governments' loan practices. My Spanish-speaking mentors in Nicaragua continue to provide inspirational leadership for our work for economic justice. We have so much to learn from them that will help us in our own economic reforms here in the U.S.

I only wish the Spanish I learned in high school, college, and studying in Saltillo, Mexico many years ago allowed me to converse deeply about these issues. I keep speaking every chance I get!

GLOSSARY

CAPTION = WE STAYED AT THE QUEEN LOBSTER IN THE PEARL LAGOON.

¡QUÉ TONTA! = HOW SILLY!
UN AVIÓN PEQUEÑO = A SMALL PLANE
EQUIPAJE = LUGGAGE
ISTMO = ISTHMUS
SALVAVIDAS = (SECOND MEANING) LIFEJACKETS
ESTUVE = I WAS
PORQUE = BECAUSE

ESPERO QUE LAS OLAS ME CANTEN DURANTE TODA LA NOCHE. = I WAIT AND HOPE FOR THE WAVES TO SING ME TO SLEEP ALL NIGHT LONG.

Day 26—Exploring

En Kakahbila, unas niñas nos recibieron en el muelle.

I had hoped to start this entry highlighting el sol shining all around me but what is really more certain is sun, sombra, viento y lluvia—probably some of all los elementos. And whether we will venture forth to Little Corn Island is unknown at this time. We might go as far as the cays for snorkeling and hammocks and birding and lunch out. Or we might go upriver to the native indigenous communities. Maybe a combination of both. Or quizás, nothing at all depending on the weather. I might just stay here—read, write and type all day long. ¿Quíen sabe? From here in this hammock on my little porch at the Queen Lobster, all possibilities sound equally enticing.

Suave, tranquilo—mi corazón—

though the sea provides no hint

del clima en la tarde.

On this little bit of Miskitu Coast,

they say this seventh day of enero

predicts the seventh month, julio.

But what does it say now

about the lit time before dusk, de ahorita?

And can the old ways ever predict anything anymore?

What will they decide is best,

today, this day, for me?

GLOSSARY

CAPTION = SOME GIRLS ON THE DOCK GREETED US AT KAKAHBILA.

SUAVE = SOFT

DEL CLIMA EN LA TARDE = OF THE WEATHER IN THE AFTERNOON

ENERO = JANUARY
JULIO = JULY
AHORITA = RIGHT NOW
MARACUYÁ = PASSION FRUIT

Richard's Passion Fruit Daiquiri Recipe

From Richard Robohm

Author's Note: The summer after returning to the U.S., we found a volunteer passion fruit vine crawling up the side of our house in Seattle and I wondered if somehow I'd brought the seed home from Nicaragua. When the harvest from the vine became magnificent, I asked Richard for his daiquiri recipe.

INGREDIENTS

(ADJUST ALL AMOUNTS TO TASTE AND TOLERANCE)
- 2 – 3 OZ PASSION FRUIT JUICE*
- OTHER FRUIT JUICE AS DESIRED
- JUICE OF 2 MEDIUM LIMES
- 1/4 TO 1/3 CUP SUGAR
- 3 OUNCES LIGHT RUM

DIRECTIONS

SHAKE INGREDIENTS TOGETHER WITH ICE.
POUR INTO 4 GLASSES (WITHOUT THE ICE).
DRINK AWAY!

*YOU HAVE TWO OPTIONS FOR MAKING MARACUYÁ JUICE:

1) YOU CAN WRING ALL THE JUICE OUT OF THE SEEDY PULP BY TWISTING IT IN A SOCK OR POCKET OF STRONG PLASTIC SCREENING MATERIAL. I GET THE MOST JUICE PER PASSION FRUIT THAT WAY. A CHINOISE WILL WORK, BUT NOT AS WELL. YOU CAN'T SQUEEZE THE JUICE AND PULP THROUGH THE MESH OF A CHINOISE AS WELL AS YOU CAN BY WRINGING A SOCK.

2) YOU CAN PUT THE JUICE, PULP, AND SEEDS IN A BLENDER. THIS WILL MAKE TINY BITS OF ALL THOSE SEEDS, WHICH YOU CAN MOSTLY REMOVE BY STRAINING THROUGH A FINE SIEVE.

SEE WHAT WORKS BEST FOR YOU. THE IDEAL MARACUYÁ JUICE AND PULP EXTRACTOR HAS YET TO HIT THE MARKET, SO WE ARE FORCED TO IMPROVISE.

Day 27—To Bluefields

Un mural sobre la vida de la comunidad

Some of the activities I've enjoyed most when in Nicaragua have been my visits to the coffee co-operatives in the mountains near Matagalpa. Twice I have stayed in a casita alongside a family's home in La Pita and twice in a casita in La Corona. These simple dwellings were built with the help of NGOs from other countries. They provide enough space for three beds with mosquito netting on a concrete floor. They also have a simple bathroom (in La Pita that is—in La Corona, guests are asked to use the family's flush toilet). In both communities, the surrounding countryside is gorgeous. Most of the time, I've visited when coffee is being harvested. It is fascinating to see the process first-hand and to participate in picking los granos de café. When I left Matagalpa, I was disappointed that this visit had not included some time in a co-operative community.

But our foiled trip to the islands allowed for a visit to una comunidad. We did eventually pile into the boat for a trip out towards the cays but were turned back at the "coast guard" station. Apparently, a panga had capsized the day before and it was too risky to send us into "the blue sea." We decided to go to Kakahbila instead and enjoyed a walk through the pueblo midday when everything was hottest.

Our guide told us several times that our destination, "the one the Norwegians helped us build," was 400 meters ahead. We learned that the villagers in the indigenous towns of the Pearl Lagoon Basin made a point of clearing their towns of trash one day per week. We did not visit on this day. All in all, it was discouraging—a chance to see just what poverty looks like in a village that is dependent on the sea for its livelihood and now suffers the effects of climate change as the dry season becomes shorter and shorter. Even though a facility had been built in hopes of attracting tourists, the town can only be reached by boat and requires a substantial time commitment from potential visitors. Day trips that do not require overnight lodging seem more realistic to me. Kakahbila was just too far away.

For our last morning in the Pearl Lagoon, Lynn and I decided to walk to the nearest towns of Raitipura and Awas and had been told that this jaunt would take 30 minutes. I was delighted to be introduced to Don Florencio Archibald who serves as the morning watchman at the Queen Lobster where we were staying. Pedro, the Queen Lobster's Spanish owner, explained that Florencio would be walking home at about the time we wanted to go to Awas and could serve as our guide for the favor of una propina. As it turned out, Don Florencio has served as the volunteer co-ordinator of Awas for the past 16 years and speaks English, Creole, Miskitu and Spanish fluently. During our two mile trek to first Raitipura and then nearby Awas on the concrete road built with help from the Danish people, we asked Don Florencio every question we had.

We learned that the volunteer leadership for the community is composed of a council, a syndicate (responsible for decisions about the land) and a judge. We learned that 25% of a person's income is used for taxes, an amount that is evenly divided between the community, the municipality, the region and the country. We confirmed that all 5 to 14-year-olds are expected to go to public schools where they all wear uniforms. Mr. Archibald showed us a marvelous morning. When we got to his town, we could not have been more pleased. Almost all of the children were in school. A new breakwater had been built recently (with support from the Danish, again). There was very little trash around and the breeze blew pleasantly off the water.

We talked with citizens who work on the cruise ships. Even though they spend many months away from home to provide for their families, these individuals seemed to prosper in terms of material goods when compared to their neighbors. In contrast to Kakahbila, I could imagine a group coming here to visit as it is much easier to reach. While the poverty is still evident, the spirit of family and living respectfully close to the land was evident.

Later we had the decidedly awkward experience of being the big pig Americans. We surmised that we could avoid discomfort on the panga trip back to Bluefields by buying 4 tickets instead of 3, spending $8(US) each instead of $6(US) each. This would guarantee us a full bench to ourselves. When we left Pearl Lagoon, I was glad to see that the front bench was completely open, suggesting that our choice had not denied another person a seat on this boat.

But ten minutes outside of Pearl Lagoon we stopped to pick up a family that included seven adults and one baby. I noticed that they spoke in Creole to the driver while pointing to our bench. He must have explained that we had paid for the entire bench because the family settled, two behind us with the driver, one propped up on the luggage and the baby on the lap of one of the women on the front bench. With the noise and wind and surf and a steady merciful sun beating down on us, I had a chance to think about this situation. I wish we had discussed it more beforehand and agreed that when we choose to travel with the public, we'd travel like the public does.

Just because we can afford to buy an extra seat doesn't mean we do. At least when it became obvious that more seats were needed we could have graciously offered up some of our bench, even though we had technically bought the space.

It's an interesting business, being wealthy enough to travel here among the materially poor. It's healthy to stop every now and then and ask, "How do I continue to be a guest here?"

I am so very grateful that as the water and electricity came and went, sometimes on and sometimes off at the Queen Lobster, we all made the best of it rather than insisting on the conveniences we take for granted in the EEUU.

Also, the loud music at the bar/restaurant beside our cabins represented business for the dueños. I am glad we didn't complain or insist on quiet when we were ready to turn in for the evening. It's always better to make suggestions anyway, like posting that the music will be turned off or cut way back at a certain time each evening. I wonder if I'll make the opportunity to talk with my travel companions about my ponderings or not.

Guests and Hosts

By Joyce Hedges

Author's Note: The following excerpt was written by one member of the first St. Mark's Transformational Travel group and initially published in Saint Mark's newsletter, The Rubric, Spring 2011.

... How does a guest behave? What is the job of a host? Do North Americans miss something when they succumb to their natural tendency to serve as a host when they visit a developing country? Can we move from generosity to community? ... It was noted that church groups from the

United States often come to developing countries to give material goods or expert advice and place themselves in the host role.

We went to Nicaragua in hopes that as listening guests we might gain a greater understanding of another culture. Our process placed equal value on laughing with the children we met, sharing a plate of 'gallo pinto' (rice and beans), and allowing ourselves to take in the harsh realities of life for most Nicaraguans. According to the World Bank, Nicaragua is the second poorest country in the Americas, behind Haiti. That translates to life on $2 per day.

We encountered 90 individual Nicaraguans, sometimes in our stumbling Spanish and sometimes with the help of a translator. We were welcomed into coffee farm kitchens to share food prepared over a wood fire and to listen to one another. In rural La Pita, the women who organize a small tourism project said ours was the first group that wanted a true conversation. No previous visitors had ever asked for a session to exchange questions and answers about one another. It felt like a breakthrough.

GLOSSARY

CAPTION = A MURAL ABOUT LIFE IN THE COMMUNITY

CASITA = LITTLE HOUSE
LOS GRANOS DE CAFÉ = COFFEE BEANS
PUEBLO = TOWN
DUEÑOS = OWNERS

Day 28—Posada de la Abuela, Laguna de Apoyo

READING/WRITING/SWIMMING = LEYENDO/ESCRIBIENDO/NADANDO

TIP OF THE DAY: **PONDER.**

La Posada de la Abuela, Laguna de Apoyo, esta ubicada entre Masaya y Granada.

I am sitting here leyendo y escribiendo on the tiled patio outside mi cabina en La Abuela's. Again there is a stiff brisa, thus no bug can light on me. I am looking out over the Laguna de Apoyo, a natural lake several miles across that has collected over the years in a volcano's crater. Una jaula gigante beside me holds tiny parakeets who are chirping continuously.

I am back in the land of Spanish as I know it—Nicaragua as I know it. Mi conductor and I were able to chat in Spanish as we made our way here even after my week trying to communicate in English-Spanish-Creole-Miskitu on the coast. I have now gone nadando for the second time on this trip:

once in the Caribbean and now in Laguna de Apoyo. Okay, I guess there was a third time when I capsized getting into the kayak at El Ranchón.

This is the sensation of dying and going to heaven—I was welcomed here as if they really know me, "Penélope!"—because I always end my trips to Nicaragua here, two nights near Masaya and close enough to the airport. Last night Maria Esperanza, true to her name, called to assure me that both transfers had been confirmed. El conductor would pick me up at the airport and deliver me to La Abuela's and then el conductor would pick me up early Sunday morning. I was surprised how relieved I was to hear this. Any temptation to reschedule my flights and head home to Rob and Seattle on Friday vanished. As usual, all would be well.

Before parting, Lynn and I had a chance to talk about buying the extra ticket for our return panga ride, the one that bought us that full bench while others were more crowded in the front and back of the boat at the expense of our comfort. Lynn and Richard came to Nicaragua four years ago, newly-retired and after a week's tour with their church group, working to provide fresh water in pueblos. It was a fairly sudden, idealistic re-location when they moved to Matagalpa. They were seeking a last adventure while healthy and strong in a place where their experiences and talents as physician and engineer might benefit the local people.

I admire their pluck and recognize that this type of pulling up roots is unlikely in Rob's and my future—unless one of our kids moves to the hinterlands, I suppose, and we follow suit. Until now, because I am still working, we've chosen only to visit our kids...let them get away first, then settle, whenever and wherever that may be. We've been together 35 years, Lynn and Richard for seven and our adventures take different forms.

One thing they've learned is that it's important to maintain their health and sanity and sometimes that means paying for comfort. Lynn recognized the tremendous resources she and Richard and we wealthy citizens de los EEUU enjoy. Living in another country (them) and even just visiting one repeatedly and staying with families (me) and trying to get a deeper sense of how most of the world lives, inevitably lays bare just how privileged we are, by no effort of our own. How to balance this scale is a quandary. Yes, we rolled with the punches when the electricity and water came and went. But we also enjoyed air conditioning and hot showers at the Gran Arabas when back in Bluefields on our last night.

This afternoon I read the cookbook that Miss Nuria Dixon sold us as we left Pearl Lagoon yesterday, *Pearls from the Lagoon, Short Stories and Recipes* by Vicki Basman. Proceeds benefit the indigenous communities we visited including Kakahbila, Raitipura and Awas. Complete with gorgeous photos of smiling, relaxed people who are talented fishermen and cooks, this story tells the tale of a people willing to welcome us, extranjeros, into this mix and share their culture and way of life openly.

Dueños Nuria and Pedro expressed their appreciation that we were tranquilos, not bent out of shape about the inconveniences and lack of utilities ready and working well at our beck-and-call. Sadly, quizás this is not the calm response they have come to expect from wealthy tourists? Hell, we had rundown whenever we wanted it. This delicious seafood/coconut stew is named because the juices run down your arms … also called "fling-me-far" by some, as per Wikipedia—definitely appropriate as I certainly did feel far flung out there in Pearl Lagoon. Who could ask for more?

Interestingly, when we drove up to La Abuela's, I found myself crying. The beauty of this resort clinging to the side of a volcano, dipping its toes into una laguna and continually washed by the wind, overcame me. When receptionist Paola greeted me, she apologized that since la electricidad no funciona, the Wi-Fi wasn't working. And later in my exquisitely-appointed cabina in the middle of an ecological reserve, complete with air conditioner (por supuesto, no funciona) and kitchenette (non-functioning coffee maker and mini-fridge), I had to laugh when I noticed the bucket of water and dipping pail in the shower. Nearly four weeks ago when I arrived at Marlene's during the dry season and noticed a similar set-up en mi ducha, she was nice enough not to startle at my ignorance when I asked about these unusual shower utensils.

"Cuando no haya agua, puedes usarla del inodoro," she explained. Now I know and will never need to ask again. With this gorgeous natural environment all around, friendly people and a resourceful attitude, one can "get by" quite nicely. The least I can do, privileged like I am, is accept the gracious hospitality that's offered as a grateful guest in someone else's home and country.

Hope. Esperanza.

By Ruth Harbaugh

Author's Note: Ruth Harbaugh and I traveled to Nicaragua together in 2012 and she has been crossing the globe in between working at home ever since. Here's what she submitted from the traveler's trail.

Three years after traveling with the Saint Mark's team, I am walking el Camino de Santiago in Spain. As I walked today, I reflected on what I realized in Nicaragua and have been consolidating in my mind and heart ever since: I stand on the side of Hope—La Esperanza.

What is hope? ¿Qué es la esperanza? I believe that hope and despair, though seemingly opposed, are in fact two halves of the same circle. Though Latin America has faced an undue share of injustice, brutality and despair, our reception was overwhelming with hospitality, commonality, culture and love. Despite the history of citizen oppression and exploitation, we met Nicaraguans who resiliently chose to remain hopeful: someone looking in a field for an herb that might cure a cut instead of lamenting that the pharmacy is out of medicine; men and women who bravely built a cooperative coffee farm to sell a valuable crop in a sustainable way on their own terms; a fully female-led fair trade clothing company that creates and sells quality goods empowering all the women involved.

Though we easily could have been seen as the face of the oppressors, our Nicaragun hosts welcomed us freely and graciously, as brothers and sisters.

Why should they do that? How could they overcome the bitter roots of anger, despair, and injustice and see us as one with them?

I believe it comes down to hope. Hope that as friends, sharing a common humanity, we may find a bond of love and understanding that transcends borders, politics and history. Though our fellow American countrymen committed heinous crimes against their soul and soil, our Nicaraguan friends choose to embrace us as brothers and sisters and share the best of their land and hearts. Why is that? After our charla, I asked the Marxist revolutionary lawyer, Dr. Ruiz, about this. I stated that I know that I come from the side of the historical oppressor, how can I really be of help?

He paused, slightly smiled with Buddha-like wisdom and told me, "Mi amiga, our nationalities don't matter—as humans, if we believe in hope, we are all in a row boat together. Though we keep rowing towards the distant sunrise together and sometimes it seems like we have lost our way, when we look back at the disappearing shore, we are encouraged to see how far we have actually come. Each of us is a candle and as one of our flames grows shorter, we light a new person's wick to keep the flame alive. We are all one."

Though injustice, strife, oppression and global battles for power will always exist, we have the ability to choose the side of hope, or choose the side of despair. As humans, it is our duty to illuminate, encourage and collectively move forward towards the light of love and justice together in whatever ways we can. My Nicaraguan family's sacred and beautiful gifts of forgiveness, acceptance and cooperation will forever compel me to choose the side of hope.

GLOSSARY

CAPTION = GRANDMOTHER'S INN AT APOYO LAGOON IS LOCATED BETWEEN MASAYA AND GRANADA.

POSADA = INN
JAULA GIGANTE = GIANT CAGE
CONDUCTOR = DRIVER
NO FUNCIONA = DOESN'T WORK
POR SUPUESTO = OF COURSE
EN MI DUCHA = IN MY SHOWER

CUANDO NO HAYA AGUA, PUEDES USARLA DEL INODORO. = WHEN THERE IS NO WATER PRESSURE [TO FLUSH], YOU CAN USE IT IN THE TOILET.

CHARLA = A TALK

Day 29—A Day of Rest and Reflection

Desayuno nicaragüense muy rico

For almost ten years, I have been very clear about learning Spanish. Y poco a poco, mejoraba. But en realidad, after turning 50 I realized I didn't want to learn it the same old American way. Instead I want mostly to work directly with native Spanish speakers and without texts. I want the lessons to be tailored individually to me. I want to learn like a baby does by listening and practicing and in context. As the decade unfolded, more and more opportunities presented themselves. I met Maria and Alfredo. I was invited to join David and others to travel to Nicaragua. My children became fluent speakers when they lived in Latin America and I traveled to visit them. I began working with toddlers y sus padres and witnessed el desarrollo del idioma first-hand.

Over and over again I was encouraged as my Spanish slowly improved and I recognized this avocation might become vocational for me. It certainly fit en mi trabajo as I worked in Head Start sites and around our diverse school district where more and more families are learning English as a second language and 30 por ciento or more of all the families I see speak Spanish fluently.

I have been very discouraged off and on. This task requires such patience of me. It is not immediate. As Clarke suggested gently when we Skyped the other day, "Mom, maybe it is harder to learn in middle age." I don't think it's the nature of my brain that holds me back but rather I think it's a reflection on my other compromisos. I am only willing to be here for four weeks. I prefer coming during the dry season. I love my home and my work and my husband and I want to live there most of the time.

As the year turns I have postponed my usual reflection practice of reviewing 2014. This is una tarea por hoy that I'm looking forward to. I also hope to finish reading and understanding the first ensayo in Pablo Antonio Cuadra's *El Nicaragüense*. Entonces, lo leo en voz alta as maestra Maria is always suggesting. I will also take mi diccionario to meals so I can look up words like "agregar," as I did when talking with Paola, la recepcionista over desayuno. Yes, it's awkward to stop a conversation to thumb through and find my new word but there are lovely people here who will allow this.

And as I write, I realize there are people like this at home, all around me—Alfredo, Annel, Annie, Giselle, Libe, Maria, to name a few—en mi iglesia y en mi trabajo who are walking diccionarios because they are native speakers and bilingual. They know mi compromiso to learning Spanish and will put up with my Spanglish en route. One option is always for them to speak Spanish and me to speak English. I want to ask which they prefer.

I could also commit to ten new words per day and reading an essay each week. It seems sabio to get a cita con un genius at the Tienda Apple to figure out this contraseña problem y para agregar un diccionario electrónico a mi teléfono. And Diana showed me a good way to read un ensayo—first scan to find and translate vocabulario nuevo, then read silently for meaning and then again en voz alta por acento y fluidez.

What about los verbos? How will I continue to attack and learn them? Quizás un ensayo every other week and a chapter of verb conjugations every other week?

Tal vez me pueda comprometer con planes específicos o tal vez no. Afortunadamente mi español de principiante regresa cuando estoy inmersa en un lugar donde todos hablan español. Entonces mi español mejora y tengo el coraje de preguntarle a mi amigo Daniel, "¿Como se dice 'con deleite?'" y como un regalo, me lo dice.

Speaking Spanish at Home

Author's Note: As my trip to Nicaragua neared the end, I found myself thinking about how I would continue using my Spanish when I returned home. I am fortunate to attend a new mission iglesia once or twice a month near my home in Seattle, Our Lady of Guadalupe Episcopal Church. The philosophy of this growing congregation is presented on their website:

www.ourladyofguadalupeseattle.org.

Our Lady of Guadalupe Episcopal Church is

+A Bicultural-Bilingual Latino-Anglo Progressive Anglo-Catholic congregation in an urban location in Seattle.

+A "destination congregation" located at this time in St. Paul's Episcopal Church in Queen Anne.

+An Episcopal community that brings together various groups seeking a healthy progressive and inclusive place to practice their faith.

+A place for those who share some connection with the Spanish language, culture, life experience and spiritual traditions.

Homily

By John Daugherty

On August 30, 2015, 20-year-old John Daugherty preached at Our Lady of Guadalupe Episcopal Church before the baptisms of one young adult and two babies. He spoke first in English then in Spanish as he went along.

... The baptismal covenant, the vow that we are about to affirm, is a promise to live the legacy that Jesus left us when he was crucified and resurrected. All the individual oaths are meaningful and related directly to Jesus' teachings, but two of them in particular are relevant to today's Gospel reading. We will swear to "proclaim by word and example the Good News of God in Christ," and to "seek and serve Christ in all persons, loving [our] neighbor as [ourselves]."

... El Pacto bautismal, el voto que estamos a punto de afirmar, es una promesa de vivir el legado que nos dejó Jesús cuando fue crucificado y resucitado. Todas las promesas individuales que haremos son significativas y relacionadas directamente con las enseñanzas de Jesús, pero dos de ellas en particular son relevantes para la lectura del Evangelio de hoy. Juramos "proclamar por palabra y ejemplo las buenas noticias de Dios en Cristo," y a "buscar y servir a Cristo en todas las personas, y amar a nuestro prójimo como a nosotros mismos]."

These two promises reference two of Christianity's most important concepts, the Good News of Christ, and Christ's New Covenant. Boiled down to basics, the Good News is that if we follow Jesus' lead and live within Jesus' New Covenant, which is to love each other as he loved us, all will be well.

Estas dos promesas hacen referencia a dos de los conceptos más importantes del cristianismo, las buenas noticias de Cristo y el Nuevo Pacto de Cristo. Yéndonos a lo más básico, las buenas noticias son el seguir a Jesús y vivir en el nuevo pacto de Jesús, que es amarnos unos a otros como él nos amó, y si lo hacemos todo irá bien.

Today's Gospel reading deals with heavy subjects: defilement and hypocrisy.

La lectura del Evangelio de hoy trata temas muy fuertes: la impureza y la hipocresía.

Jesus says that, contrary to the dogma of the Pharisees, it is not what someone puts into himself that defiles, but what they put out. I interpret this to mean that it is not what I do to myself that determines my morality, but what I do to others. Because what goes into me does not affect anyone else, but what comes out (words and actions) has the power to affect someone positively or negatively, depending on whether I compliment or insult, hug or punch.

Jesús dice que, contrariamente al dogma de los fariseos, no es lo que alguien pone en si mismo lo que contamina, sino lo que uno pone hacia fuera. Yo interpreto esto para decir que es no lo que me hago a mí mismo lo que determina mi moralidad, sino lo que hago a los demás. Porque lo que me entra no afecta a nadie, pero lo que sale (palabras y acciones) tienen el poder de afectar a alguien positiva o negativamente, dependiendo de si hago algún complemento, insulto, abrazo o golpeo a alguien.

GLOSSARY

CAPTION = VERY DELICIOUS NICARAGUAN BREAKFAST

POCO A POCO = LITTLE BY LITTLE
MEJORABA = IMPROVED
EN REALIDAD = IN REALITY
EL DESARROLLO DE IDIOMA = DEVELOPMENT OF LANGUAGE
EN MI TRABAJO = AT WORK
POR CIENTO = PERCENT
COMPROMISOS = COMMITMENTS
UNA TAREA = A TASK
ENSAYO = ESSAY
LO LEO EN VOZ ALTA = I READ IT OUT LOUD

AGREGAR = TO ADD
RECEPCIONISTA = RECEPTIONIST
IGLESIA = CHURCH
SABIO = WISE
CITA = MEETING
TIENDA = STORE
CONTRASEÑA = PASSWORD
ELECTRÓNICO = ELECTRONIC
TELÉFONO = TELEPHONE
NUEVO = NEW
ACENTO = ACCENT
FLUIDEZ = FLUENCY

TAL VEZ ME PUEDA COMPROMETER CON PLANES ESPECÍFICOS O TAL VEZ NO. AFORTUNADAMENTE MI ESPAÑOL DE PRINCIPIANTE REGRESA CUANDO ESTOY INMERSA EN UN LUGAR DONDE TODOS HABLAN ESPAÑOL. ENTONCES MI ESPAÑOL MEJORA Y TENGO EL CORAJE DE PREGUNTARLE A MI AMIGO DANIEL, "COMO SE DICE 'CON DELEITE?'" Y COMO UN REGALO, ME LO DICE.= PERHAPS I CAN COMMIT TO SPECIFIC PLANS AND PERHAPS NOT. FORTUNATELY, MY ROUGH SPANISH RETURNS WHEN I AM IMMERSED IN A PLACE WHERE EVERYONE IS SPEAKING SPANISH. I AM DELIGHTED THAT MY SPANISH IS BETTER. AND THAT I EVEN HAD THE COURAGE JUST NOW TO ASK MY FRIEND DANIEL, "HOW DOES ONE SAY, 'DELIGHTED?'" AND, LIKE A GIFT, HE TOLD ME.

Day 30—Flying Home

Adiós, Nicaragua Nicaragüita, país de amor y muchos colores.
Espero verte pronto. (Foto de Bre Domescik)

I am comfortably seated on a Delta flight flying to Atlanta. Esta mañana, el conductor Roberto y yo nos encontramos a las cinco y media, muy puntual. He drove me to the airport in less than an hour, while un otro guía de su companía, Tierra Tours (out of Granada), explained Nicaragua's fascinating history to me en español. Guía Gustavo was going to el aeropuerto to meet "dos V.I.P.'s de India por un tur de Managua." I only had to ask him to re-explain a brief part of the history in English. My last 200 pesos were well spent on una propina for these two—one $C100 bill to Gustavo and one to Roberto.

Throughout my time in the airport, I found myself wondering if Nicaragua had improved servicios turísticos magnanimously in the less-than-five years since my first visit in 2010 or if my comfort level had increased exponentially. I did overhear a conversation another traveler had with a vendedor confirming the improvements. One thing has remained the same: a beautiful poem by Matagalpino, Ruben Darío, installed in the middle of the airport en palabras y escultura. Estos bustos de mujeres are placed in a circle on pedestals. A verse about each woman is engraved on the pedestal below her. These cabezas represent all the peoples del mundo who have mixed their sangre together to create today's linda gente nicaragüense.

Truthfully I have already started promoting the next connections. Via Facebook, two friends have expressed an interest in mi consejo for their viajes a Nicaragua. I have sent messages to amigos who might be interested in buying a home en Matagalpa that I know will be listed on the market soon. Plus, I am returning with a draft of this booklet, hoping to interest others in learning Spanish.

Maybe I'll really stand on the bridge and create a study tour for a group of miembros de mi familia and friends from my church and office. Talk about motivation for continuing to learn. What would I advise my fellow travelers as they prepare for such a tour?

Top Ten Tips

10.   Consider limiting yourself to one electronic device only, and only using Wi-Fi briefly when it's available.

9.   Look less flashy (por ejemplo, leave diamond ring/fancy watch at home).

8.   Bring crisp dollar bills for spending money (torn bills may not be accepted.)

7.   Pack lightly and bring a flashlight/headlamp.

6.   Wear shoes all the time, including flip-flops in the shower.

5.   Wash hands frequently (or use hand sanitizer when no running water is available.)

4.   Bring a water bottle and drink water incessantly (bottled or filtered only).

3.   Por lo menos, learn people's names. Write them down or ask people to write them down so you don't misspell and can remember. This is the first connection point. Even if you know no other Spanish words, know names. Repeat them. In Nicaragua, consider greeting folks with a kiss on the left cheek which is similar to the handshake we use here.

2.   Stay curious.

1.   Breathe deeply whenever you think of it.

Want to join me la próxima vez, amigo mío? ¡Ojala!

Facing Suffering Alongside

Author's Note: I wrote this piece in August 2015. It supplements Day 30 because on that day I was heading home. I was on the bridge. I was considering how I could bring all of this learning about language and culture home with me. For me, loving our neighbors through encouragement is one of the best ways to "bridge." In my judgment, it is despicably sinful to do otherwise.

This morning from my porch in Seattle, I watched a Facebook video of an older white woman yelling all-but-obsenities at a middle-aged Latina woman in the line at a fast food restaurant. She ranted imprecise, crazy statements about freedom of speech and Nazism and "we" wanting only English spoken here in the U.S. My friend from Our Lady of Guadalupe Episcopal who posted the clip prefaced his post with a brief description of the similar verbal lashing he had endured. He had experienced this lashing earlier in the day in public in our free country of vast diversity, built by immigrants—after the indigenous people were beaten back, that is. I found myself speechless, utterly, dismally sad, wanting to stand alongside in dismay. Commenting with a sad, weeping emoji seemed woefully insufficient in the face of such ugliness.

Maybe I will remember this at 1 p.m. today when I am tempted to stay home and read the thick, seductive Sunday paper here in this comfortable leather rocker while I contentedly observe the sweet summer world around me. Instead, I can decide now to go to la misa in the hopes of hugging, embracing, enfolding my friend or simply being in his presence in prayer for a few minutes. I want to assure him there are many, thousands, millions of us Anglos who are dizzyingly proud of him for speaking two languages fluently, for enduring whatever pain and suffering the triumph of learning English entailed and continues to require of him.

Bless him especially, Lord, and the others who face such malignancies due to the fact of their grand bilingual talent and courageous examples.

GLOSSARY

CAPTION = GOOD-BYE NICARAGUA, LITTLE NICARAGUA, COUNTRY OF LOVE AND MANY COLORS. I EXPECT TO SEE YOU SOON. (PHOTO BY BRE DOMESCIK)

ESTA MANAÑA = THIS MORNING
NOS ENCONTRAMOS A LAS CINCO Y MEDIA. = HE MET ME AT 5:30.
MUY PUNTUAL = RIGHT ON TIME
UN OTRO GUÍA DE SU COMPANÍA = ANOTHER GUIDE FROM HIS COMPANY
EL AEROPUERTO = THE AIRPORT

DOS V.I.P.'S DE INDIA PARA UN TUR DE MANAGUA = TWO V.I.P'S FROM INDIA FOR A TOUR OF MANAGUA

200 PESOS = 200 CÓRDOBAS
SERVICIOS TURÍSTICOS = TOURIST SERVICES
PALABRAS Y ESCULTURA = WORDS AND SCULPTURE
ESTOS BUSTOS DE MUJERES = THESE BUSTS OF WOMEN
CABEZAS = HEADS
DEL MUNDO = OF THE WORLD
SANGRE = BLOOD
LINDA GENTE NICARAGÜENSE = BEAUTIFUL NICARAGUAN PEOPLE
MIEMBROS = MEMBERS
AMIGO MÍO = MY FRIEND
¡OJALÁ! = GOD WILLING

✪ After ✪

Mi perra, Roxy

In late May, Rob and I took our dog Roxy to the beach for a final visit. We would rather have stayed on that particular bridge en la playa forever because there we created a sweet bubble for our puppy's last days. We fed Roxy roasted chicken, scrambled eggs and ground beef by hand that weekend because she wouldn't eat the same-ol-same-ol anymore. She was only reluctantly trying this good stuff and Rob was the best caregiver of the two of us. After the ER vet found the tumor on her lung in the dark hours one morning and gave us the dreaded explanation about why Roxy's breathing was so labored, she also gave us prednisone. Maybe with this boost from modern medicine Roxy would rally or at least be able to eat her favorites. We had opted for no more major poking and prodding though and certainly no more separation from her tribe—Rob and me—until the ultimate end when all the yellow labs in heaven along with our grand ol' cat, Bucky, would welcome her.

I was reminded of when my father died a couple of months after I returned from Nicaragua. Long ago, when Dad told me he was receiving hospice care, he mistakenly called it "hostage care." But after his death, I tried to explain why he had not been a hostage during those many months. He had rallied, my sisters and the community helped and my mother somehow had served—with the assistance of many—as his caregiver until he died. His last tricycle rides—with my Mom and his oxygen tank in tow—were in late December when I was away. But I was able to be present at the end and was alongside him when he breathed his last. As it does, time stood still when he died and in that peaceful holiness that passes understanding, I was amazed at the sheer shimmering stillness.

Next, I imagined that possibility for our sweet pooch. We did not hold her hostage long. She wasn't even wagging her tail at the end and one morning she just didn't get up. She couldn't.

This writing project helped get me through that next stretch in surreal land, the inevitable experience when a loved one dies. Of course I couldn't do much more than put one foot in front of the other for a while but the manuscript took on a life of its own. My dear friend and fellow Nica sojourner, Jeanne, read it through and reported in with encouragement. I shared my photos and captions with Maria and my circle of adult Spanish learners. And there have been other Spanish-related tangents. For instance, Annie checked my translations of some frequently-used work documents so I could use them with parents and colleagues as needed. Alfredo and I designed a Second Sunday Summer Series at Our Lady of Guadalupe

Episcopal Church. Even though the alliteration in the name of the formation classes didn't hold up in Spanish, I realized I could continue learning the language at Our Lady, no long flight required.

The bridge between English and Spanish extends and I don't have to leave home to walk across it. Yes, el puente is solid, between Life and Death too. I can live here on it or I can cross to either side whenever I like. After all, I know there is really only a very thin line that separates any of us. Y bendiciones abound.

Esta Noche—24/6/15

Author's Note: The summer after my dad and my dog died, we visited Clarke where he was teaching in Spain. I wrote this poem en route.

Esta Noche—24/6/15

Esta noche en Sevilla I will see mi hijo
for the first time since my Dad died.
They share a name and many characteristics.

Esta noche flying to Seville
I dreamt of my Dad for the first time
since then.

¡Sweet Jesús mío!

GLOSSARY

CAPTION = MY DOG, ROXY

EN LA PLAYA = AT THE BEACH
BENDICIONES = BLESSINGS
ESTA NOCHE = THIS NIGHT
24/6/15 = 6/24/15
JESÚS MÍO = MY JESUS

APPENDIX A:
Nicaragua at a Glance

Population:

5.4 million, growing at 2.7% per year

Area:

120,254 sq. km., slightly smaller than the state of New York

Ethnicity:

77% Mestizo, 10% Spanish/European, 9% Black, 4% Native Indigenous

Employment and wages
- Nicaragua is the 2nd poorest nation in the Western Hemisphere.
- 65% of population is un-and-underemployed.
- Less than 25% of the economically active population has the security of a fixed salary.
- 68% of those employed earn less than the basic cost of living.
- 13% drop in the purchasing power of salaries in 2007—the most drastic in the past eight years.
- Four out of every ten people live on less than $1.00/day and about 3 out of every 4 (75.8%) live on less than $2.00/day.
- An estimated 909,571 extreme poor in 2001 has now risen to 2,224,814 in 2008.
- Extreme poverty increased 140% from 2001 to 2007.
- The Nica rural population: 30.5% poor and 70.3% extreme poor.
- The Nica urban population: 30.9% poor and 6.7% extreme poor. WB 2008

Food Security
- Average plate of food (rice, beans, tortilla, meat) costs between 30-50 córdobas ($2.00--$2.50).
- Rise in food prices in Nicaragua have increased 45% over the last nine months.

- Rice has doubled in price, price of corn tortillas up 54% from Jan. '07 to Jan. '08.

Education
- According to the Ministry of Education, there are over 500,000 children not in school.
- Twenty-one out of every 100 children leave school in the first grade.
- Only 35% of preschool-age children are in school.
- Average education level is 5.6 years—only 3.6 years in rural areas.
- Only four out of ten children enroll in high school and only 40% of those graduate.
- Teachers earn only half the average salary of the rest of Nicaraguan's workers.
- Only 60% of those who enroll in primary school finish—out of the 87% that enroll.
- 33% non-literacy rate, one out of every three Nicaraguans is non-literate.

Health
- Infant mortality rate: 30 per 1,000 live births.
- 27% of public school students suffer from chronic malnutrition.
- Anemia is 25% at the preschool level and 35% in 5-year-olds—anemia has serious consequences on cerebral development.
- Without a free daily snack provided to 1 million school children, many would eat only once a day, as it provides 30% of children's nutritional needs.
- 55% of Nicaraguans don't have access to basic medicines.
- The number of doctors per 10,000 Nicaraguans has decreased from 6 to 3.8 since 1996. In the U.S. (2003) there are 26.6 doctors for every 10,000 people.

Migration

- An estimated 800,000–1,000,000 Nicaraguans live in Costa Rica permanently or seasonally; an estimated 500,000 Nicaraguan immigrants live in the United States.
- Remittances have steadily increased each year reaching $990 million in 2007.

Basic Services

- Electricity coverage is less than 50% of the country.
- 84% of the rural population has only one of the three basic services—potable water, access to a toilet/latrine, and electricity. 57% of the rural population has none of the basic services.
- Only 48% of rural sector has access to potable water, and 77% of families in extreme poverty lack access to potable water.
- 10% of roads are paved.
- Electricity coverage is less than 50% of the country.

Science & Research

- Nicaragua invests only 0.1% of its GDP in research and development (below Latin American median of 0.5% and far below UNESCO's recommended minimum of 1%).
- Nicaragua accounts for 27 articles per year in the SCI (scientific publications database), while Costa Rica counts for 10 times more (285), and Mexico 300 times more. The average number of scientific researchers per million people in Latin America in 250; Nicaragua has just 20 or 25.

APPENDIX B: 2014 Annual Report about Use of Resources Contributed by St. Mark's Cathedral

Prepared by: Marvin E. Chavarría M. (marvin@aglobal.org.ni)

I. GENERAL INFORMATION

Aldea Global (Global Village, in English: www.aglobal.org.ni) began in 1992; it is a Not-for-Profit Civil Association of Small Producers. However, it is not without means for growth!!! In 1996 Aldea Global was given legal status under Law 147 and given the number 107 by MIGOB or the Government Ministry for Perpetuity. Aldea Global is located in Jinotega, Nicaragua. We work with more than 2,355 small producers (1,649 men and 706 women) organized into 20 ALDEA (Village) committees in 70 rural communities in the north central region of Nicaragua, in the counties/parishes/regions of Jinotega, Matagalpa and Esteli.

VISION: To be a valuable organization for the progress of our rural families.

MISSION: We, Aldea Global, will be consistently in support of our small producers leading to profitable farm and service enterprises. We will be in harmony with God and the environment, placing high value on social responsibility and gender equality.

VALUES:

HARMONY WITH GOD = Work together with Love and Peace.

HARMONY WITH THE ENVIRONMENT = Care for natural resources of the earth and build societal awareness of the necessity for this care.

SOCIAL RESPONSIBILITY = Improve quality of life in the ALDEA family.

GENDER EQUALITY = Men and Women share equally in rights and responsibilities.

II. GROUP OBJECTIVE

With the funds provided by Saint Mark's Cathedral, we propose to benefit directly the wives and children of male associates and women who decide on their own initiative to collaborate with Aldea Global (Global Village). With the fund, priority will be given to women who are less likely to acquire credit from the official bank of the country.

What are our ALDEA Committees?

They are bodies or structures that make up Aldea Global, constituted by productive areas, district- or micro-regions according to the designation of each municipality, for the direct execution of the programs, businesses and projects of the Association. They support the role of the Board of Directors and facilitate communication among the more than 2,355 members with their management organizations and with the local governments to exercise the process.

III. BACKGROUND

Aldea Global and St. Mark's Cathedral initiated a working alliance to benefit rural women who have the capacity to become profitable except for their socioeconomic condition that does not give them access to loans through the formal Nicaraguan bank. Our institutions share values and objectives that permit synergy that helps the economic development of rural women in Jinotega, Nicaragua. Between 2009 and 2014, St. Mark's Cathedral helped create access for these women to small loans. The Fund totals $13,500(US), which grew in the following manner:

Description	Year	Concept	Amt USD
First trip from St. Mark's Cathedral to Jinotega, Nicaragua	2009	Seed Capital	10,000
Second trip from St. Mark's Cathedral to Jinotega, Nicaragua	2010	Donation to fund	500
Third trip from St. Mark's Cathedral to Jinotega, Nicaragua	2012	Donation to fund	500
Fourth trip from St. Mark's Cathedral to Jinotega, Nicaragua	2013	Donation to fund	500
Carolina's Donation	2013	Donation to fund	500
Seattle's Donation	2014	Donation to fund	1,500
FUND TOTAL			13,500

With the St. Mark's Cathedral Fund, we developed small economic initiatives directed and organized across Solidarity Groups (SG) initially made up of women and men. In 2009, we began with 14 Solidarity Groups (SG) principally working to produce basic grains and small businesses. In 2010, with the new Credit Policy of Aldea Global, they organized calling themselves Women's Groups for Business Development (WGBD). These WGBD were made up solely of women producer associates. The women in WGBD demonstrated an excellent culture of repayment and have taken advantage of opportunities provided for undertaking their activities. These are needed to better the quality of life in their families.

The women who make up WGBD, besides having access to loans, also get to move forward making family decisions. Some are elected to Aldea Global committees which allows them to also be candidates to run for Aldea Global's Board of Directors. Also, they participate in other organized expressions of a community and municipal nature.

Aldea Global has negotiated other funders to join with St. Mark's allowing in 2012 the disbursement of $40,133.18(US) in loans to 148 women organized in 26 Solidarity Groups. In that year, $7,118.72 was provided by the St. Mark's Fund to 36 women. By December 31, 2013, Aldea Global had disbursed loans totaling $31,857.84 to 130 women organized in 29 WGBD. In that year, $7,436.27(US) was provided by the St. Mark's Fund. The financial activities supported: small businesses, vegetable production, coffee and basic grains (corn and beans).

IV. ADVANCES AS OF December 31, 2014

On December 31, 2014, the business center credit disbursed loans worth a total of $35,358.07(US) to serve 131 women. Out of this total, they have received $6,513.04 and December 31, 2104, the remaining balance to be repaid equals $28,845.01 (see table 1).

Table 1. Total disbursements and balances for loans to women as of December 31, 2014

Type of Credit	Total amount of funds Aldea Global and C. San Marcos		
	Number of People	Disbursed Funds	Outstanding Balances
WGBD	107	19,011.22	17,365.79
Individual	24	16,346.85	11,479.25
Total	131	35,358.07	28,845.04

Of the 131 women served by Aldea Global, 54 women were served by the St. Mark's Fund. The financial activities were: small businesses, purchase of land and bean production (see table 2).

Table 2. Balance of Loans made only from the St. Mark's Cathedral Fund as of December 31, 2014

Businesses	Number of Women	Credit balance in St. Mark's Fund
Small business	50	9,980.88
Land	1	3,899.37
Beans	3	587.59
Total	54	14,467.84

Of the total credits mentioned above, the St. Mark's Fund financed 54 rural women, who at the close of 2014 have a balance of $14,467.84 (see tables 2 and 3).

Table 3. List of Groups and Women Helped by the St. Mark's Cathedral Fund as of December 31, 2014

Name of Business	Name of Client	Identity Document*	Balance
WGBD Dios Bendiga	Alba Rosa Orozco Alaniz		229.78
	Ana Celia Cruz Contreras		229.78
	Maryure Sulema Pérez Pineda		229.78
Sub Total WGBD Dios Bendiga			689.33
WGBD EL Esfuerzo	Araceli Del Carmen Rizo González		96.04
	Brígida Del Socorro Quezada Quezada		96.04
	Judelka Del Rosario Altamirano González		96.04
	Silvia Ramona Hernández		96.04
Sub Total WGBD EL Esfuerzo			384.14
WGBD Jehová es mi Pastor	Apolonia Orozco		44.17
	Edis Maria Villlagra Chavarría		51.29
	Liliana Del Carmen Villagra Duarte		35.50
Sub Total WGBD Jehova es mi Pastor			130.97

Name of Business	Name of Client	Identity Document*	Balance
WGBD Medalla Milagrosa	Beatrís Del Carmen Rizo Estrada		227.46
	Deisi Esperanza Dórmus Monzón		132.68
	Marbelí De Jesús López		227.46
Sub Total WGBD Medalla Milagrosa			587.59
WGBD Mujeres Dispuestas del Dorado	Alba Ilenia Díaz Rivera		27.97
	Judith Lisbeth Rodríguez Canales		27.73
	María Del Socorro Díaz González		27.97
Sub Total WGBD Mujeres Dispuestas del Dorado			83.68
WGBD Mujeres Emprendedoras de Pantasma	Aracely Del Carmen Herrera Cantarero		62.50
	Etel Jael Hernández Villagra		36.81
	Guadalupe Delfina Espinoza		30.68
	Yerli Damaris Montalván Rodríguez		36.81
	Yorleni Yuniet Ríos Hernández		18.39
Sub Total WGBD Mujeres Emprendedoras de Pantasma			185.19

Name of Business	Name of Client	Identity Document*	Balance
WGBD Mujeres Emprendedoras del Dorado	Ada Marisela Salgado Rivera		224.61
	Arelis María Cruz		90.75
	Janeth Del Carmen Chavarría		224.61
	Rosa Emilia Méndez Herrera		224.61
Sub Total WGBD Mujeres Emprendedoras del Dorado			764.58
WGBD Mujeres Unidas en el Comercio	Cruz Del Rosario Martínez Estrada		36.27
	Danila Genoveva Gómez García		13.21
	Reyna Isabel Hernández		38.09
Sub Total WGBD Mujeres Unidas en el Comercio			87.57
WGBD Sagrado Corazón de Jesús	Andrea Vargas Joxquin		40.55
	Leonor Del Socorro Espinoza González		34.98
Total WGBD Sagrado Corazón de Jesús			75.53
Sub Total – only credits with WGBD			2,988.59
Individual Credits	Aura Lylian Romero		318.52
	Aura Rosa Méndez Monzón		63.22

Name of Business	Name of Client	Identity Document*	Balance
	Cristina Del Carmen Picado Castro		751.13
	Domitila Del Carmen Palacios		2,814.90
	Eveling Zeneyda Calero Gutiérrez		97.99
	Fátima Del Rosario Pérez Castro		241.27
	Fátima Rosa Gutiérrez		100.47
	Florentina Del Rosario Bucardo		134.57
	Gerónima Del Socorro Gutiérrez Montenegro		172.76
	Haydee Del Carmen Valle García		748.03
	Idalia Moran Gómez		83.55
	Ivania Dolores Chavarría Estrada		129.83
	María Aminta Zelaya Cantarero		61.94
	María Dolores Benavidez Rivera		61.41
	María Elena Cruz		182.31

Name of Business	Name of Client	Identity Document*	Balance
	María Elena Méndez Monzón		67.55
	Maribel López Rivera		62.30
	Maritza Del Rosario Valle Palacios		123.91
	Nidia Del Socorro Herrera Andino		119.59
	Reyna Isabel Centeno		497.32
	Rosa María Romero Rivera		249.50
	Rosa María Pineda López		3,899.37
	Rosario Del Carmen Palacios Altamirano		123.91
	Teófila Ramona Rizo Palacios		373.93
Sub Total of Individual Credits			11,479.25
TOTAL GENERAL			14,467.84

*Numbers removed for security purposes

Appendix C: Early Childhood Spanish-English Glossary

Vocabulario general—General Vocabulary

LA ADOLESCENCIA—ADOLESCENCE

LOS ATAQUES EPILÉPTICOS—SEIZURES

LA AUTOAYUDA—SELF-HELP

LA AUTOESTIMA—SELF-ESTEEM

EL/LA BUEN ALUMNO/A—GOOD STUDENT

LAS DESTREZAS—SKILLS

LA DISCIPLINA—DISCIPLINE

EMBARAZADA—PREGNANT

ESTAR ENFERMADO/A—TO BE SICK

ESCRIBA SU NOMBRE EN LETRAS DE MOLDE, DESPÚES PONGA SU FIRMA Y LA FECHA.—
PRINT YOUR NAME, THEN YOUR SIGNATURE AND THE DATE.

LAS FUERZAS—STRENGTHS

LAS HABILIDADES—SKILLS

LA INCAPACIDAD—DISABILITY

LA INHABILIDAD—DISABILITY

LA INTERVENCIÓN TEMPRANA—EARLY INTERVENTION

"MAMA LEONA"—"MAMA BEAR"

EL NÚCLEO FAMILIAR—NUCLEAR FAMILY

PRE-ESCOLAR—PRESCHOOL

PRE-ESCOLAR DE DESAROLLO—DEVELOPMENTAL PRESCHOOL

LA PRIMARIA—ELEMENTARY SCHOOL

EL/LA PRIMERIZO/A—FIRSTBORN

EL RETRASO—DELAY

LA TARDANZA—DELAY

TEMPRANO, MEDIO O TARDE—EARLY, AVERAGE OR LATE

LAS VENTAJAS—ADVANTAGES

Los Sustantivos—Nouns

LOS APUNTES Y BOCETOS—NOTES AND SKETCHES

LA PIZARRA—BLACKBOARD

EL BORRADOR—ERASER

EL CANGURO—FRONT BABY BACKPACK (LIKE A KANGAROO)

EL CEREBRO—BRAIN

LOS COLORES—MARKERS

LOS CRAYONES—CRAYONS

EL CUADERNO—NOTEBOOK

EL CUADRO—PICTURE

LA CUENTA—BILL

EL CUENTO—STORY

LOS COLUMPIOS—SWINGS

LA ESCUELA—SCHOOL

EL GORRO—CAP

LOS JUGUETES—TOYS

EL LÁPIZ—PEN

EL LÁPIZ DE GRAFITO—PENCIL

EL LÁPIZ DE CARBÓN—PENCIL

LAS MARCADORAS DE COLORES—MARKERS

LA MOCHILA—BACKPACK

EL NACIMIENTO—BIRTH

EL/LA NIÑERA—NANNY; BABYSITTER

EL NIVEL—LEVEL

EL PAÑAL—DIAPER

EL PÁRRAFO—PARAGRAPH

LA PINTURA—PAINTING

LAS VACUNAS—IMMUNIZATIONS

EL VIAJE DE CAMPO—FIELD TRIP

Los verbos—Verbs

AGREGAR—TO ADD

AMAMANTAR—TO NURSE (A BABY)

ARRASTRARSE—TO CRAWL

BORRAR—TO ERASE

CANTAR—TO SING

COLORAR—TO COLOR

CONTAR—TO COUNT, TO TELL

CRIAR—TO RAISE

DIBUJAR—TO DRAW

DISFRUTAR—TO ENJOY

DIVIDIR—TO DIVIDE

MECER—TO ROCK (A BABY)

PEDIR—TO ASK FOR

✹ Notes, Sources and Permissions ✹

Author's Note: Every attempt was made to contact the individuals and publishers whose work is included in this book. If unpublished, permission to use was granted by the creator in person or in writing. Any piece including photos not otherwise identified is by the author.

Cover
Cover Photo: Arjen Roersma, "Ernesto and Nohelia on Rio Tapasle Bridge," Near Muy Muy, Department of Matagalpa, Nicaragua. Used with permission from Arjen Roersma, Director of Matagalpa Tours.

Gratitude Gathering
Photo: Bre Domescik, "Granos de Café." Used with permission from Bre Domescik.

Why This? Why Now? Why Not?
For more about code switching, see Nilep, Chad. "Code Switching," Sociocultural Linguistics. Colorado Research in Linguistics. Vol 19. (Boulder: University of Colorado, 2006).

Illustration: Rob Reid, "When I Was a Guest in Nicaragua." October 2015. Used with permission from Rob Reid.

Before
Essay: Ana Mesenbring, "Nicaragua—From the Eyes of a Teenager," *The Rubric* (Seattle: Saint Mark's Episcopal Cathedral, Spring 2011). Used with permission from the Very Reverend Steven Thomason, Dean of Saint Mark's Episcopal Cathedral and Ana Mesenbring.

Day 1—Traveling
Excerpt: David Mesenbring, "Memorandum to Saint Mark's Episcopal Cathedral Church in the World Coordinating Committee," October 12, 2009. Used with permission from the Very Reverend Steven Thomason, Dean of Saint Mark's Episcopal Cathedral and the Reverend David Mesenbring.

Day 2—Managua

Prayer: "El Padre Nuestro," (Libro de Oración Común, p 286.)

Prayer: "The Lord's Prayer," (Book of Common Prayer, p 364.)

Day 3—Marlene's House and Colibrí School

Sermon: David Mesenbring, "A Cure for Blindness," (Seattle: Saint Mark's Episcopal Cathedral, December 12, 2010). Used with permission from the Very Reverend Steven Thomason, Dean of Saint Mark's Episcopal Cathedral and the Reverend David Mesenbring.

Day 4—Interlude

Photo: Bre Domescik, "La Pita, Nicaragua, December, 2010." Used with permission from Bre Domescik.

Essay Excerpt: Clarke Reid, "Adiós," Un Americano en Andalucía (Pozoblanco, Andalucía, Spain: I.E.S. Los Pedroches, Spring 2014). Used with permission from Clarke Reid.

Day 5—Code Switching

Recipe: Noelia Corrales with Estercita, "Receta Tortillas de Plátanos Maduro." Summer 2015. Used with permission from Noelia Corrales.

Day 6—A Steep Path

Poem: Penny Reid, "Mi Corázon Lleno." February 2012.

Day 7—Jinotega

Essay: Carolina Reid, "Sisterhood." Fall 2015. Used with permission from Carolina Reid.

Day 8—Family Nest

Illustration: Ollie Mae Nicoll, "La Familia en Mi Casa." September 2015. Ollie and Penny traveled to Nicaragua in February 2012. Ollie is a student at the Savannah College of Art and Design. www.behance.net/olliemae (accessed September 28, 2015).

Day 9—At Yuri's Farm

Prayer: Penny Reid, "Querida Madre." Summer 2011.

Day 10—Returning to Town
Essay: Penny Reid, "Poor People?" Fall 2011.

Day 11—With My American Friends
Promotional Flyer: "Social-Cultural Tourism in Nicaragua with Noelia Corrales." (Seattle: Saint Mark's Episcopal Cathedral, April 2011). Used with permission from the Very Reverend Steven Thomason, Dean of Saint Mark's Episcopal Cathedral.

Day 12—Christmas Cookies
Letter: Noelia Corrales, "Excerpts from a Letter to Transformational Travel Team at Saint Mark's Episcopal Cathedral." April 2011.

Day 13—A Quiet Holiday
Spanish Lullaby: Public Domain, "Duérmete, Mi Niña."

Day 14—Boxing Day
Poem: Pablo Antonio Cuadra, "Coral de los poetas del alba." POESIA I. (Managua, Nicaragua: Colección Cultural de Centro America, Serie Pablo Antonio Cuadra No. 1, edited by Pedro Xavier Solis and Marcela Sevilla Sacasa, 2003), p 328. Used with permission from Pedro Xavier Solis, grandson of Pablo Antonio Cuadra.

English Translation: Sarah Hornsby and Matthew C. Hornsby, "Chorale of the Poets of the Dawn." *Book of Hours* by Pablo Antonio Cuadra, English Translation. (Academia Nicaragüense de la Lengua, Managua, Nicaragua, November 2012), p 60. Used with permission from Pedro Xavier Solis, Francisco Arellano Oviedo, Director of Academia Nicaragüense de la Lengua and Sarah Hornsby, translator.

Christmas Card: Diana Iris Herrera Castro. December 23, 2014. Used with permission from Diana Iris Herrera Castro.

Day 15—Sick
Verse: Julian of Norwich, "All Shall Be Well." In Context, Article #31. www.christianhistoryinstitute.org (accessed September 2015).

Poem: Penny Reid, "From Here Inside God, Merry Christmas!" December 2012.

Day 16—Sunday at Home
Essay: Penny Reid, "Even Dogs Die." Summer 2015.

Illustration: John R. Clarke, "Sky Jumper." November 2006.

Day 17—Week Three of Classes
Essay: Penny Reid, "Mixing Up Vowels, AGAIN!" Summer 2015

Day 18—The Basics: Water, Phone, Electricity and Money
Sales tag on weaving: "Telares Nicaragua." www.telaresnicaragua.com (accessed October 3, 2015). Used with permission from Noelia Corrales.

Day 19—New Year's Eve
Website: "La Escuela de Español Colibrí." www.colibrispanishschool.com (accessed September 2015). Used with permission from Noelia Corrales.

Day 20—Adios 2014
Essay: Penny Reid, "Pardon Me!" Summer 2015.

Day 21—Welcome 2015
Report Excerpt: "Transformational Travel Mission Purpose Statement— Saint Mark's Episcopal Cathedral Church in the World in 2011." Winter 2011. Used with permission from the Very Reverend Steven Thomason, Dean of Saint Mark's Episcopal Cathedral.

Day 22—Transitioning by the Sea
List: Penny Reid, "What a Paranoid Optimist Can Fit in the Right Purse." January 2015.

Day 23—Around Corn Island
Poem: Penny Reid, "To You of the Red Carpet." April 2010.

Day 24—Rough Seas in Paradise and in my Heart, Last Day at Al Paraíso
Website: Matagalpa Tours. www.matagalpatours.com (accessed September 2015). Used with permission from Arjen Roersma, Director of Matagalpa Tours.

Day 25—Pearl Lagoon
Essay: Betsy Bell, "Jubilee, Liberation from Debt and Poverty." August 2015. Betsy is a traveling grandma, writer and health nut who can be

reached at www.EmpoweredGrandma.net (accessed September 2015). Used with permission from Betsy Bell.

Day 26—Exploring
Recipe: Richard Robohm, "Richard's Passion Fruit Daiquiri Recipe." Summer 2015. Used with permission from Richard Robohm.

Day 27—To Bluefields
Essay: Joyce Hedges, "Guests and Hosts." *The Rubric* (Seattle: Saint Mark's Episcopal Cathedral, Spring 2011). Used with permission from the Very Reverend Steven Thomason, Dean of Saint Mark's Episcopal Cathedral.

Day 28—Hope. Esperanza.
Essay: Ruth Harbaugh, "Hope. Esperanza." September 2015.

Day 29—A Day of Rest and Reflection
Website: "Our Lady of Guadalupe Episcopal Church is:" www.ourladyofguadalupeseattle.org (accessed August 2015). Used with permission from the Reverend Alfredo Feregrino, Vicar of Our Lady of Guadalupe Episcopal Church.

Sermon: John Daugherty, "Homily—August 30, 2015." Used with permission from The Reverend Alfredo Feregrino, Vicar of Our Lady of Guadalupe Episcopal Church, Seattle, and John Daugherty.

Day 30—Flying Home
Photo: Bre Domescik, "La Pita, Nicaragua." December, 2010. Used with permission from Bre Domescik.

After
Poem: Penny Reid, "Esta Noche—24/6/15." June 2015.

Appendix A
Brief: Nicaragua at a Glance. (Washington, DC: Witness for Peace, 2008) Used with permission from Gloria Jimenez, Witness for Peace Nicaragua Team. For more infomation about Witness for Peace, visit www.WitnessForPeace.org (accessed August 2015).

Appendix B

Report: Marvin E. Chavarría M., "2014 Annual Report about Use of Resources Contributed by St. Mark's Cathedral." (Jinotega, Nicaragua: Aldea Global, January 2015). English translation by Kerry Altman, Maria Jimenez, Penny Reid and Julie Simon-Braybrooks. Used with permission from Warren Armstrong, Executive Director of Aldea Global, and the Very Reverend Steven Thomason, Dean of Saint Mark's Episcopal Cathedral.

Appendix C

Glossary: Penny Reid, Early Childhood Spanish-English Glossary. Spring 2015

Bendiciones de Paz

Excerpt: Rick Steves, "Christmas in Managua." blog.ricksteves.com (accessed November 2015). Used with permission from Rick Steves.

About the Author

Photo: Alfredo Feregrino, "Penny and Sebastian," (Seattle: September 20, 2015). Used with permission from Alfredo Feregrino.

✪BENDICIÓN DE PAZ✪

"Christmas in Managua"
Thursday, December 30, 2010 at 10:00 a.m.

For Christmas Eve, I gathered with local worshipers in the humble chapel of Nicaragua's University of Central America under hard-working fans for Mass. ...

A lanky elderly priest was greeted warmly by the congregation. He was Fernando Cardenal, one of the Sandinista priests John Paul II famously wagged his finger at during a visit to Nicaragua back in 1983 for politicizing the church. Cardenal's trouble-making message was a Liberation Theology message—that Christians are to be more than charitable. They are to ask why there is poverty and to organize to work for economic justice and dignity in the face of hunger and suffering.

The chapel was filled. It was a bring-your-own-maracas crowd, and with each song the place filled with the happy sound of these shakers. The Lord's Prayer was sung to the tune of "Sound of Silence." Before the offering plate was passed, a woman stepped out from her pew to remind everyone that Father Cardenal lives very modestly and to assure all that the offering would go to support the church's work with the local poor.

My favorite thing about a Central American Mass is the fiesta-like "passing of the peace." Every time I'm in an American church and that moment in the service comes and people solemnly shake hands, I miss the uproar that breaks out at that moment in Latin America. With mariachi energy the band plays while all attending burst into a rollicking commotion of hugging and exchange of blessings. It just goes on and on. ...

—Rick Steves

✿ABOUT THE AUTHOR✿

Penny Reid is gradually learning Spanish as children do, with others and without texts. She serves families as an early childhood psychologist in the public schools. On Sundays, when she's not at the beach or in the mountains, she is present at the Episcopal cathedral or la nueva iglesia bilingüe* near her home in Seattle. Penny lives with her husband and enjoys applauding their two adult children who communicate well in both English and Spanish. Traveling the world is a favorite activity of everyone in the family.

*the new bilingual church

I wrote everywhere in Nicaragua including on the dock beside my cabin at the Queen Lobster, Pearl Lagoon.

Escribí en todas partes de Nicaragua incluso en el muelle al lado de mi cabina a Queen Lobster, Pearl Lagoon.

Penny and newborn Sebastian get to know each other after the service at Our Lady of Guadalupe Episcopal Church in Seattle. He is already communicating. (photo by Alfredo Feregrino)

Penny y el recién nacido Sebastián empiezan a conocerse después de la misa en Our Lady of Guadalupe Episcopal Church en Seattle. El ya está comunicándose. (foto de Alfredo Feregrino)

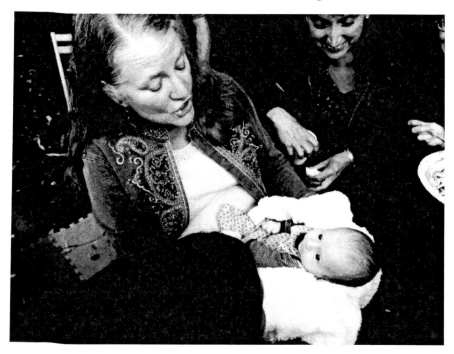